WASTED

WASTED

The Plight of America's Unwanted Children

PATRICK T. MURPHY

Chicago   Ivan R. Dee   1997

The paperback edition of this book carries the following ISBN:
1-56663-333-8

Library of Congress Cataloging-in-Publication Data:
Murphy, Patrick T. (Patrick Thomas), 1939–
    Wasted : the plight of America's unwanted children / Patrick T.
Murphy.
        p.   cm.
    Includes index.
    ISBN 1-56663-163-7 (alk. paper)
    1. Child welfare—United States.   2. Abused children—United
States.   3. Poor children—United States.   I. Title.
HV741.M85   1997
362.7'0973—dc21   97-8978

For Susan, Matt, and Joe

Acknowledgments

I can never truly acknowledge all those who helped me write this book, for they include everyone who has ever worked for me—lawyers, social workers, investigators, secretaries, and clerks. Unfortunately I cannot include the hundreds of names I should. Suffice to let those whose names come to mind now stand for the rest. These include Kim King, who has worked for our office since she graduated law school ten years ago and who is now chief deputy of our juvenile office; Rebecca Kolleng, my chief assistant in building the office; and Lee Ann Lowder, the most competent legal writer I have ever known, whose administrative and supervisory abilities help put together our office. I must also note the outstanding legal

Acknowledgments

work of our supervisors, including Ora Schub, Peter Schmiedel, Djuana O'Connor, Robert Harris, Maroba Matsapola, Yvonne Holte, Tom Grippando, Sylvia Giacomuzzi, Su Sherock, Mary Burns, Judy Tansley, and Sherry Fox, who also read this manuscript and gave me many useful suggestions.

Others who have helped our clients in the past include Paula Dwyer, Ellen O'Brien, George Stears, Marilyn Sharko, Joan Brogdon, Therese Schaefer, Miriam Solo, Patricia Collins, Cynthia R. Farenga, Susan Poth, Marsha Hayes, Diane Lopez, Denise Kane, Mary Bird, Rich Cozzola, Kathy Kennedy, and Patricia Horne.

Then there are those, neither lawyers nor social workers but just hardworking people, without whom our office could not operate. These include Antoinette Tronco, my secretary who has been with me for seventeen years since she graduated high school, and Nancy Edelman, Camelia Harper, Patricia Cole, Veronica Burgess, Anne Barrett, Ron Riley, Joe White, Dorothy DeGrange, Marie Amore, Maureen McDonald, Angela King, and Joyce Purcell.

Those who have been my mentors in the law include Jerome F. Goldberg, William J. Martin, John Cleary, Lewis A. Wenzel, Patrick J. Hughes, John Shullenberger, Martin Ganzglass, Bob McGuire, Harold Goldman, Judge Arthur L. Dunne, and one who tried to instruct me in effective writing, Father John Fogerty.

Those who have appointed me and continued my appointment as Public Guardian have endured my idiosyncratic ways with relative patience, even humor. They include former Governor Jim Thompson, Chief Judges Harry Comerford and Donald O'Connell, Presiding Judges Nancy Salyers, Henry

Budzinski, and Tim Evans, and former Presiding Judges William S. White and Arthur Hamilton. Some individuals have at times been opponents but have always acted professionally toward my office and myself, and always with a goal of achieving what is best for the children. Jess McDonald, the present director of the Illinois Department of Children and Family Services, and his predecessor, Gordon Johnson, stand out in this respect, as do Cathy Ryan of the state's attorney's office, Assistant Public Defender Darron Bowden, Diane Redleaf, formerly of the Legal Assistance Foundation, and Professor Tom Geraghty of Northwestern Law School.

I owe a major debt of gratitude to Ivan Dee, whose confidence in my work spawned this book and whose editorial suggestions have made it more readable.

I wish to recognize some of the clients I have represented. We in society have dared pushed them aside, but I have learned much from them: William N., Bernadette B., Pamela W., Frank P., Tony K., Mabel W., John B., Bobby G., Diane R., and so many, many more.

My brother Joe got me involved in this field by introducing me to the Juvenile Court while I was still in law school. Joe had a master's in social work and worked in a variety of capacities with abused, neglected, and delinquent children. He supervised the first shelter in Cook County that housed only abused children. He later became a Catholic priest and used his social work background as chaplain at the Indiana State Prison. He died too young at forty-four. The final words he wrote to my parents, brothers, sisters, and myself before he died are especially relevant here: "Pray for the men, women, and children pushed aside by society. Pray for the ones that

Acknowledgments

we dare call criminals, delinquents, mentally ill, deviated in any way. Pray for the poor, and pray for you and I who could have done better, could have done so much more."

Contents

Foreword

This book is about how a system designed to help children is instead helping to destroy them.

Robert Benchley, a popular humorist in the thirties and forties, attended law school before recognizing the absurdity of the law and turning to humor as a saner calling. While at Harvard, Benchley encountered a question on an admiralty test concerning a dispute over fishing rights between the British and the Norwegians. As with countless law students, myself included, Benchley did not know the answer. After thinking for a while, he wrote that many professors and international lawyers had discussed the problem of the fishing rights from the point of view of the Norwegians, and an equal number of learned scholars had discoursed about it from the point of view of the British. But no one had discussed the problem from the point of view of the fish. Benchley then proceeded to explain how the fish felt about being fished for by the British and the Norwegians.

With the other lawyers in my office—the Public Guardian of Cook County, Illinois, which includes metropolitan Chicago—I represent abused and neglected children and the elderly who require guardianship because of Alzheimer's, organic brain syndrome, and other mentally disabling diseases. In other words, I represent disabled individuals at both ends of the age spectrum. I represent the fish.

In court or in meetings I listen to child welfare professionals, self-proclaimed child advocates, and academics declare that the child's best interest is their only consideration. But spend time with most of them and they begin coming across like the British or the Norwegians. Most argue that the children are not really victimized by their parents' abuse but by an unjust and uncaring society which fails to help the parents, who then pass this societal abuse on to their children. Other experts are more concerned with the smooth operation of the bureaucracy and the courts.

I have represented abused and neglected children on and off since the 1960s. I have visited them in housing projects, orphanages, foster homes, bars, and even on the street where children are waving down cars trying to make a few bucks by offering sexual favors. But mostly I've seen and represented them in court. In this book I tell the stories of some of the people I have represented and some of the cases I have been involved with. (In order to protect the identities of the innocent, I have either changed the names of the individuals I write about in this book or used only their first names.)

The first two chapters deal with my early years of prosecuting felons and then representing abused and neglected children. I include these chapters to provide a perspective on the problems we face today. We thought child abuse and crime were out of control thirty years ago, but in retrospect those were the good old days. We also thought we would end poverty, only to end up today with the underclass. The remaining chapters explain how the child welfare system and the courts are dealing with the avalanche of child abuse cases produced by the wealthiest country the world has ever known. I admit that my view is that of a lawyer lost in the midst of the fray. My perspective is from the valley, not the mountaintop. My kind of experience is often scorned as merely "anecdotal" by those perched at the top of the mountain.

An editor once suggested that I write this book by bringing one family through all the problems within our juvenile justice and child welfare systems. But that approach is either dishonest or patronizing. Underclass families, like rich unhappy families, are each unhappy in their own ways, and, because they don't have much to cushion their unhappiness, they are pretty miserable most of the time.

But even their misery differs. I could take a family in a housing project and show young boys committing crimes, teenage girls having babies, and grannies heroically trying to save all of them, succeeding in some cases and failing in others. But I know in the next apartment a young woman is raising several children by different fathers and sending them to school clean and neatly dressed, not taking drugs, going to

church on Sunday, and doing an impossibly good job with exceedingly limited resources. And in the next apartment the
mom is off doing drugs every night of the week while a five-
year-old baby-sits for the two-year-old. And in the next apartment . . . well, on it goes.

I do suggest some solutions, but the reader should not expect much, for I have more questions than foolproof answers.
I have read enough books on welfare and the underclass and
have seen enough five-minute analyses on TV newsmagazine
shows to know that only a fool claims to have solutions to the
overwhelming violence, abuse, despair, and ignorance stalk-
ing our inner cities and waiting to explode into the suburban
and exurban populations.

So will the solutions I suggest make life better for most of
our clients?

No.

Might they make life better for some of our clients?

Perhaps, marginally.

Will some of these solutions make our social service systems more effective, more efficient, more humane?

I hope so.

A couple of years ago I received a call from a TV producer. She said a well-known anchorwoman was putting together a special on "Programs that Work" for children in the
so-called underclass. Specifically she referred to a case in
Chicago in which a ten-year-old and an eleven-year-old threw
a five-year-old out the fourteenth-story window of a housing
project because the five-year-old wouldn't steal candy for
them. Could I tell her what programs work for kids like those
who tossed the five-year-old boy out the window? I answered

that I knew of no programs that would help them. After a brief silence, she thanked me and hung up.

I exaggerated. Certainly some programs will benefit inner-city children. But these programs need a great many contributors. When the public schools pass illiterates from year to year until they drop out, unable to read, write, add, or subtract, we self-righteously blame the schools. But the education establishment merely provides a service five hours a day. Parents must keep their kids at home in the evenings and motivate them to do their homework and go to school the next day—and every day. And parents must be in contact with teachers to monitor their children's progress and demonstrate their own interest in their children's education.

I could have told the producer that some programs might help certain kids. After-school programs in housing projects provide a safe haven where kids can study and play. But the children who get into these programs have decent parents. The same is true for preschool programs, food programs, and so forth. But the people tearing apart our inner cities and creating an underclass are not the children of motivated parents. They are children raising themselves—sadly, and often with tragic results.

So in this brief book my story is a bleak one, and it does not have a happy ending. What I do and see every day is raw, and I'm not sure Hemingway could give it coherence. But the rawness is ripping apart the lives of underclass children today and precurses an even starker future. A few people I can point to as the "bad guys." Most neglectful or abusive parents are "there-but-for-the-grace-of-God-go-I" people who suffer from the underclass syndrome: children too young, education too little, fathers too absent, and jobs too scarce. Ultimately these burdens lead to depression and substance abuse. The tragedy is that the system frequently treats the truly evil parent no different from the unintentionally neglectful one. And while there are few bad people among the social workers, lawyers, and other professionals who work in the child welfare arena, sometimes in trying to help underclass parents we unintentionally harm their children.

In the sixties, as a Peace Corps volunteer, I lived in a so-called third-world country. In those years and since, I have traveled in Asia and Africa through much of the so-called underdeveloped world. In the sixties and seventies I worked as a legal services lawyer on Chicago's West Side, representing primarily poor people in criminal and civil actions. Nothing I saw as a Peace Corps volunteer in Africa or as a traveler in Africa and Asia comes close to matching the despair and misery that today strangles the American underclass. What was beginning to happen in the inner city in the sixties and early seventies was mild compared to what occurs now. And if what we see today is a harbinger of what will occur in years to come, our nation is in real trouble.

Like Plato's man chained to the cave wall, those of us who represent children see only the shadows of what is happening with the underclass. But I fear these shadows for several reasons, not the least of which is that the numbers of children pouring into the child welfare system has in the past eight years doubled nationwide and tripled in most of our big cities. Forces have come together to create an underclass in our major cities which is a fourth world, a culture separate, distinct, and unrecognizable to a majority of Americans, including increasingly other Americans of color.

Our child welfare system and juvenile courts, like our prisons and criminal courts, serve a disproportionate number of African Americans. Racism and segregation have spawned a black underclass in our major cities, now nurtured by conservative neglect and patronizing liberal programs. But discussions of child abuse, like those of crime, avoid this racial component of the underclass and how too many of its members, beaten down and ultimately sapped of hope, turn to drugs to get through the day. When these people and their families are destroyed, we blame the drugs. Really, it's life in the underclass that causes the destruction. In this book I try to face these issues forthrightly, as I have personally encountered them.

Children who need help and protection are stretching our governmental services to the limits. They are helpless to defend themselves, and those who should care for them are frequently the problem rather than the solution. Because this urban mess has grown so quickly, society, government, and the courts have not yet figured out an appropriate response. Much of our assistance is obsolete, even counterproductive.

If we do not begin to resolve these problems, they will overwhelm us. Before we can begin to grapple with these new realities, we must understand what is now happening with the very young, particularly children of the underclass. Since I represent them, I cannot excise my own bias. But at least I can assure you that the story is told from the point of view of the fish.

WASTED

On a hot and muggy 1989 afternoon I faced a wiry little fellow whose dark eyes darted from the papers he read past my head to the men and women thronging the small courtroom behind me. Every seat was filled, and people were standing in the aisles, cramming the sides, and making the already heavy air fetid. Society gave the little man in front of me a black robe and an elevated seat to accentuate his authority and impartiality. But the crowd didn't want impartiality, they wanted my head. He didn't disappoint them.

He spoke slowly, enunciating every syllable: "As Senator Barry Goldwater stated some two and one half decades ago, a statement which fairly well describes the actions taken by our Founding Fathers, and I quote, 'Extremism in the defense of liberty is no vice. Moderation in the pursuit of justice is no virtue.' Now, who can deny the ring of truth these words convey. Moderation in the pursuit of justice is no virtue. I would think that all men who love freedom and justice would not hold these words lightly."

Glaring at me, he continued, "But there are always men who strive to subjugate their fellow man. Men who seek power for the sake of power. Men who seek public office for the power to forge them and for their own personal gratification and self-aggrandizement, and then, without hesitation, use that power to dominate and subdue their fellow man."

Two years earlier, as Public Guardian, I had taken over the representation of abused and neglected children in Cook County. The office that had previously held this responsibility had never appealed or in any effective way challenged a judge's decision or that of the state bureaucracy responsible for providing substitute care for abused children. But we challenged court decisions and filed a number of civil rights actions against the state's child welfare agency (the Illinois Department of Children and Family Services). Worse, from the perspective of the judges and bureaucrats, we went to the media to expose some of the court's more egregious cases and practices.

None of this went over very well with some of the judges and child welfare bureaucrats accustomed to carrying on business protected by confidentiality laws. Several came down hard on our lawyers. The judge now reading his opinion while occasionally looking up to glare at me was the prime protector of the status quo and our harshest critic. He routinely belittled our lawyers. Once, when I argued a case, he threatened to lock me up if I had the audacity to utter one additional word. Recognizing that discretion is the better part of valor, or perhaps having seen the inside of too many lockups while interviewing clients, I took his advice.

After trying to reason with the judge, I decided to request a

*change of venue in every new case filed before him. In Illinois
a lawyer has a right to one substitution of judge, or change of
venue, in each case. Since my office represented nearly every
child, and since that judge heard only abuse and neglect
cases, we were effectively putting him out of business. He
recognized this and, in a courtroom packed with his
supporters, read his forty-page opinion denying our motion.*

*The judge compared himself to those who opposed the
Nazis in Germany and slave owners in this country. Lest the
subtlety of comparing me to Nazis be lost on the social workers
and lawyers wedged into the courtroom, he became specific.
"The petitioner, Mr. Murphy, has spun a conspiracy of
mischief. He has assumed a posture of omniscience and
infallibility. . . . He has engaged in tactics and stratagems so
unprofessional as to be unworthy of any lawyer. . . . He has
chosen, instead, to pursue this sad and foolish vendetta, and
to embark upon this senseless course of action aimed at
rendering this court powerless to fulfill its legitimate
functions."*

*He concluded, "Are we to act honestly and fearlessly, to
promote justice and serve the public interest, or are we to
cultivate an obsequious and fawning visage at the end of a
supple spine, fearful, lest some angry lawyers see fit to charge
us with irrationalities against which we may not defend? Are
we to wear our robes as badges of honor, proudly and with
dignity, as we are about our business of doing justice, or are
these robes to be transformed into shrouds of shame, disgrace,
and dishonor, behind which we cringe and tremble, hiding our
cowardice, fearful less some petty tyrant see fit to hurl at us
some mindless accusations against which we may not*

*defend? . . . If this is to come to pass, and pray God it does
not, then we had best exchange our black robes for yellow
ones, for that color would better suit our positions and
characters."*

The lawyers, social workers, and other child welfare types
erupted into spontaneous, emotional, and sustained applause,
shouts, and even whistles. Trying for anonymity, I slunk past
the smirking, slick-looking, mostly young men and women
and out the courtroom. I'll appeal the son of a bitch, I thought
to myself, and get even with every last fucking one of you.
(After three appeals, we did.) But at that moment I was also
trying to figure out how I got myself into this situation in the
first place. Mogadishu. That's it. I blame those goddam
Somalis. . . .

1

A THIRD WORLD INITIATION

The equatorial sun had just sunk into the horizon, and soft ocean breezes whisked away the steamy residue as I walked from the main police headquarters to a tea shop straddling Mogadishu's main road. Eight or nine tables were scattered along the side of the road next to a small hut from which waiters served a syrupy substance called tea along with greasy rounds of fried rice and camel meat. It was December 1966, the holiday season. Not that there was much celebrating in

Mogadishu except by a few heathens like myself. And I wasn't much in the mood for celebrating.

About a year earlier, on a whim, I had quit my job as a prosecutor in the Cook County state's attorney's office and joined the Peace Corps. I had just sent another colored fellow (they were not to be black for several years or African-American for several decades) to jail for some now-forgotten offense and had returned to my office. Falling into a hard wooden chair, I swiveled around and stared out of a window probably last cleaned during JFK's campaign. The snow outside was made grey by soot belching from the tall chimneys of nearby factories. During my reverie I thought about Robert Frost, then the poet of the hour, and his poem about the road less traveled. A couple of hours later I phoned the Peace Corps. A pleasant man informed me that three countries were looking for lawyers. Indeed, the training program for one, Somalia, was about to begin.

A year later, sipping my tea, I watched nomads herding their camels down to the wharf where Arab dhows would take them to Saudi Arabia, ultimately to be someone's main course. I was beginning to figure out why most people choose the roads *more* traveled. Those less traveled may be so for good reason—they go nowhere. The blur of camels, nomads, and townsfolk in brightly colored outfits and the traditional Somali bickering (the English were not complimentary when referring to Somalis as the Irish of Africa) swirling around me had once seemed like a romantic tapestry. Now they pounded at me like a toothache.

Initially I worked for the minister of justice in Somalia, helping to coordinate the criminal code of the newly independent country. The south had been colonized by Italy, the north by the British. Neither foreign power had made much of an impact beyond a couple of towns where the nomads passed through to trade. After independence, someone, probably a United Nations expert, decided to combine the English procedural code with Italian substantive law. This made no sense from the point of view of the English or the Italians, and seemed particularly foolish to the Somalis who had a perfectly sensible common law hammered out by their elders over centuries.

It didn't take me long to figure out that the Somalis were better off without the expertise of the English, the Italians, or myself. So I moved over to the National Police Building and worked for the commander of the national police force, a kind of carabiniere. The police were exceedingly polite. They gave me a motor scooter, an office, and, being fairly intelligent, pretty much ignored me. For good reason: there wasn't much of a crime problem. The Somalis had no real tradition or history of violence. Arguments between members of different clans were settled by elders. During the year before I went to work for the police, there were only six documented homicides in the entire country, and all of these involved fights at water holes about whose camel could sip the water first. I traveled all over the country and walked Mogadishu's dusty roads and was never hassled. (Since that time, of course, the Somalis have moved into the forefront of civilization, using bullets, machetes, land mines, and starvation as effective tools of population control.)

About this time it hit me that I wasn't doing a damn thing for the Somalis. They should throw out the Italian and English codes and integrate their ancient customs into a written code as soon as they could put together a written language—which they were not to have until four or five years after I left the country. Nor did I have anything to offer the police, whose job it was to arrest thieves and help settle clan disputes when they weren't cozying up to the CIA operatives who were teaching them how to wiretap their army brethren, most of whom belonged to a different tribe and were being taught by the Soviets to wiretap the police.

Ultimately the Soviets won, and the army "saved" the nation from its democratically elected president. Two years after I left, my old boss was put under house arrest while a dictator, Siad Barre, incorporated what he had learned from the Soviets to spy upon, incarcerate, and shoot Somalis he didn't like—and who didn't like him.

I wasn't to realize for decades that my Somali experience was positive. Not for the Somalis, for me. Being ripped from a South Side white working-class Chicago neighborhood and dropped into a sea of blacks, from a Catholic Christian pre–Vatican II tradition into a Muslim one, and from an Irish-American ethnic tradition into a nomadic culture, shocked me. I never looked at the world in quite the same way again.

But that recognition was also years away. In Somalia, amidst that brightly colored blur, I ruminated about the frustrations and silliness of what I was doing and also about the frustrations and silliness of the job I had left to seek satisfaction in this barren land halfway around the world.

I had worked my way through college and law school running elevators, opening doors for rich, snobby folks on Lake Shore Drive, and guarding corpses in the morgue during the school year while digging tunnels or skipping along girders as a construction laborer during summers. College was boring, law school deadly. The state's attorney's office was a release from prison.

I started out prosecuting concealed guns, gambling, and prostitution cases. The concealed guns were carried by fragile-looking older black men and women and burly truck drivers for protection. Most cases were tossed out because of a bad search. No one went to prison. I never saw a gangster, lout, or thug carrying a concealed weapon. The folks the cops hustled in for gambling were quiet, well-dressed, middle-aged, working-class black men and women, pushing what we called "policy" (the numbers game, it was called elsewhere). They made a modest, unspectacular living off it until the state took it over, made it legal, called it Lotto, and made winning almost impossible.

By day I worked hard keeping Chicago streets safe from law-abiding black folks; by night I went voluntarily to the Criminal Court building on Chicago's West Side to write appellate briefs. All this activity had the hoped-for result of attracting the attention of my superiors. Just three months after joining the office, I was promoted to the criminal trial division—in record time, I was told.

But if I broke a record getting into the felony trial division quicker than anyone in the modern history of the office, I probably also broke one getting out. Along with other assistants, I sent a lot of thugs to prison, even asked for the chair. The jury found the man guilty but refused by one vote to execute him, which was probably better since his appeals would still be pending. But it wasn't the romance that you see in the

TV law shows or read in the crime novels. In the first place, most of the louts were black, though in those days we had our share of poor whites and Hispanics. Instead of craftily planning their victim's demise, most murderers blew away strangers in barroom confrontations, or friends, wives, or lovers because of jealousy, booze, or, increasingly, drugs. Contradicting a host of eyeball witnesses, granny, mom, auntie, or girlfriend would assure the jury that Mr. Defendant was home reading poetry or watching TV or getting laid. Mostly white or all-white juries usually chose to believe the eyeballs.

The ferrety-looking rapist seldom got away with it. The manly-looking fellow who claimed that the lady consented usually did go free, the bruises and black eye being explained away as foreplay. Women who claimed that an acquaintance or friend had raped them were scorned. Pornographers were arrested and their grainy sixteen-millimeter porn movies confiscated, to be viewed Friday afternoons by hooting, booze-swilling prosecutors and judges. In the early sixties a well-known comedian, Lenny Bruce, was prosecuted for using obscene language in a Chicago nightclub. The naughty word, which the otherwise foul-mouthed prosecutor refused to say in front of the jury because it would offend his mother, rhymed, he pointed out, with truck. While the jury deliberated Bruce's guilt or innocence (and guilty it would be), the prosecutors and other lawyers in the building huddled together in the judge's chambers watching a confiscated porn movie.

No big-time drug dealer ever got caught. The "big-time" sellers were usually skinny little runts with needle marks up and down their arms, legs, stomachs, just about anywhere, selling for another user to support his habit. They were usually turned in by a previously reliable informant who was a user who got nabbed and was not the least bit reliable. One of our best informants, Teddy H., used up just about all his veins and was shooting into his penis. He would have turned in his mom, wife, kid, priest, you name it, to stay in the street.

Not that any of this bothered or bored me. In fact, like most green twenty-six-year-old kids, I found it rather exciting—for a while. But before long my youthful exuberance ran smack into the reality around me. Every day dozens of inmates, mostly black, trooped from their grim cells and were herded through the bleak tunnels separating the County Jail from the Criminal Court building to lockups behind the courtrooms, ultimately to be prosecuted, defended, and judged by white males.

Don't get me wrong: I cannot claim prescient political correctness. Nor was I, am I, one of those who claim that the many black men clogging our prisons are innocent. After all, someone out there is shooting poor blacks, holding them up, burglarizing their homes, and raping their women. Several years later, interviewing these men as a defense lawyer, for a while I almost swallowed the conspiracy theory. But it didn't take long to discover that the soft-spoken guy in the lockup was not the same fellow in an alley behind a bar at two in the morning. (Years later I woke up to discover that the quiet adult reasonably explaining his or her actions to social workers, judges, and lawyers could also be the bully, high on crack or booze, facing down an out-of-control two-year-old.)

But why this disproportionate number of mean, vicious black thugs? And what were we accomplishing? Had it been any different in 1936? (Indeed it was a little different. There were more white thugs then.) Or would it be any different in 1996? (It turned out it would be different: the number of blacks in the system would be greater.) Along the way it dawned on me what was going on. It was the other young lawyers and myself who were making real progress. I was not yet twenty-seven, a pretty fair trial lawyer and getting better, learning my trade on the backs of all these mopes. We would move on to become middle-class attorneys, maybe judges, maybe even rich because of these experiences. And these guys would go to prison and come out and probably go back again and come out and end up being broken old men who would lead meaningless and wasted lives.

Then our sons and daughters or younger siblings would one day gain experience by prosecuting and judging and defending and maybe teaching or probationing or social working the kids of these guys, and learn their trade, and move on to . . .

So ultimately I lost the stomach to send these men to prison, and here I was in Mogadishu having lost my stomach to proselytize the results of my education and experience to the Somalis.

Late in the evening I left the tea shop and slowly negotiated the ocean road until I arrived at the Lido, a blue stucco building just yards from where the Indian Ocean pounded the rocks below at high tide. The Lido was one of a few watering holes in that overwhelmingly Muslim country. Not that the Somalis were orthodox in their religious views. They adapted Islam to fit the needs of their nomadic way of life. Pigs would be a nuisance to herd, and booze would get in the way of long treks.

After a small entryway, the interior of the Lido consisted of a dimly lit, barnlike room with tables arranged around a circular dance floor. A bar was at one end and a stage at the other. A Somali band turned out pretty horrible renditions of "I Wanna Hold Your Hand" and other contemporary hits.

Somali men hunched at tables, furtively scanning the room to see who might be watching them sipping beer, looking for all the world like middle-aged American guys at a Times Square porno shop. And just like the porno shop, there were lowlife Somalis who didn't care who might see them. These fellows were interested in women, smuggling, gambling, or one or more of the illegal activities going on around us every evening. Russian sailors, Italian expatriates, UN bureaucrats, and young men from the diplomatic corps rounded out the male patrons dancing and drinking beneath fans that slowly pushed the stale air around the room. Only Sidney Greenstreet and Humphrey Bogart were absent.

By day Somali women wore traditional brightly colored garments which clung to their bodies from one shoulder to their feet, leaving the other shoulder and part of a breast bare. By night the hostesses at the Lido wore dresses skimpy even by 1967 Western standards. Brief skirts and sleeveless blouses exposed dark, shiny, pulsating bodies. The hostesses were more than that, but they were not prostitutes either. They danced gratuitously and like all Somalis would chat and argue for hours over just about anything. They were available, of course, but that was not necessarily part of the equation.

I met a few friends, Somalis and others, and drank and

danced with my friend Asha, and argued about America's racial attitudes. The Somalis were not sophisticated enough to grasp the concept of freedom of speech for idiots. Why would we tolerate louts whose pictures they saw in the local paper and on the sides of the Soviet and Chinese embassies confronting Martin Luther King in Chicago and holding signs reading, "Niggers go back to Africa," and "Monkeys go back to your trees"?

Finally the band left, my friends went home, and Asha joined the other hostesses on their way to someplace or other. The Lido closed, and I walked along the ocean away from town. I stumbled for hours along the beach and small rocky cliffs bordering the ocean, ultimately settling on a large rock and staring at the black ocean. At the distant horizon it was beginning to turn blue as the rays from the not quite rising sun played upon it. As the sun emerged, I turned and in the distance saw a white speck and four blobs of brown which, in half an hour or so, resolved themselves into a nomad with white flowing robes and four camels. He approached and stopped about a first down away, a tall, angular black nomad from one of the world's poorest nations facing a blond, husky young man from one of the richest. We stood facing each other as moments seemed to merge into minutes. Finally I said, "Nabat" (Peace). He responded in kind, waved, and moved on, ultimately becoming a white speck and four blobs of brown. I had a vision of Zorba and the young man clasping hands amidst frustration and despair and dancing on the beach.

I didn't dance. I walked back to Mogadishu and told the director I was returning to Chicago.

2

LEARNING THE SYSTEM

When I left for Somalia men wore suits with narrow lapels, skinny ties, button-down white shirts, and wing-tipped shoes; women wore nylons, garter belts, skirts, and dresses below their knees. A loose woman on the first date might French-kiss. Women in professions were rare, and those few generally were not taken seriously by anyone, particularly other women.

When I returned, ties were wide and clownish, pants narrow at the hip and wide at the shoe, and shirts psychedelic. Skirts barely covered the essentials, and panty hose made garters anachronistic, at least until Victoria's Secret discovered men's secret yearnings. Women were flocking to professional schools as the feminist movement gathered steam.

The sexual revolution was in full bloom. Men and women met at parties, smoked a joint, and hopped into bed with strangers without regard to yet unheard-of diseases such as chlamydia, herpes, and AIDS. The sexual revolution finally met its demise not on the shoals of these diseases but because of the embarrassment and then the boredom of waking up with a foul-smelling stranger who, in the harsh light of day, over coffee and a bun, was not quite the royalty he or she appeared to be after a bottle of wine and a couple of joints the previous evening.

I joined up. My hair grew long, I sported a beard. I drove a Ducati motorcycle and lived in a three-and-a-half-room flat next door to the No Pets Allowed bar. On more than a few occasions I took too much of the grape and grain both at that bar and others.

Like countless other relatively young men and women, I wanted to contribute to society, to help bring down institutions and mores that made people poor and powerless. Although we couldn't know it at the time, these were the good old days when there were still more young black men in school than in prison, and when inner-city public schools graduated more than half their students. But we were going to make things better. And indeed the civil rights movement succeeded in making life much better for most minorities, particularly those in the middle class. With respect to the desperately poor, the underclass, we failed. Some argue that our efforts greased the way for today's problems. I don't think so. But some of the programs, some of the *poor-as-victims* philosophy—reinvented today in *It Takes a Village*—may have played a role.

I used the skills I had picked up as a prosecutor to help criminally accused indigent defendants. They deserved adequate representation, still do, but in those days many considered them victims of a police conspiracy rather than men and women charged with a criminal offense and deserving a decent defense. Most of us did not go that far, but we did believe that but for their poverty they would not be facing the vagaries of the criminal justice system. Or, as Anatole France put it a hundred years ago, "The law, in its majestic equality, forbids the rich as well as the poor to sleep under bridges, to beg in the streets, and to steal bread."

I once represented three young men, seventeen and eighteen years old, all high school dropouts. The cops claimed they had shot up the apartment of some other kid who wore a different-colored tam. Whoever did the shooting—and if it wasn't my guys it was three other fellows from the same gang—missed the young man with the wrong-colored hat. Instead they blew out the brain of his three-year-old brother. Ultimately the jury exonerated my clients, but during my many visits at the County Jail I got to know them pretty well. One, I'll call him Tony, stood out. He had a superior intelligence and a photographic memory. A fellow I knew referred him to Dartmouth, which ultimately offered Tony a no-strings-attached full scholarship. Actually there was a string or two attached: the kid had to stay out of jail. He didn't. Several weeks before he was to leave for Hanover, he and a couple of buddies held up a service station. Tony may have been smart enough to get into an Ivy League college but not smart enough to avoid the cops, who arrested him as he stepped out of the store with the loot in his hand. He got three years at Statesville Prison. He's dead now, I've heard.

It didn't take many victories like this to convince me to redirect my energies. I joined the cutting edge of the Great Society and headed up a small storefront Legal Services office on the West Side, not far from Juvenile Court. Legal Services was—is—a federally funded corporation giving money to programs to provide legal services for the poor. A great idea. Like a lot of Great Society programs, it was decimated by the Republican revolution of the nineties. But revolutions seldom are spawned in vacuums, and Legal Services is a good example of a program that needed the support of the very people it often attacked in its class-action lawsuits, the politicians.

In the beginning, Legal Services lawyers saw their role as representing poor folks needing a divorce, or fighting a landlord stingy with the hot water but generous with the rats and roaches, or just confronting some stonewalling, self-important contentious bureaucrat or miscreant merchant. For the most part, that's still the case. But some lawsuits took on government agencies. For example, during the late sixties and early seventies I litigated successful civil rights suits against the Illinois departments of Public Aid, Corrections, Mental Health, and Children and Family Services. The fact that many of these cases, even when won, had an almost negligible impact upon the real problems or the clients was irrelevant. Government and politicians do not like those who rock the boat.

Some Legal Services lawyers avoided clients and pre-

ferred class actions. For one thing, a few minutes of convers-
ing with a poor woman needing help with her stingy-with-heat
landlord left most of us needing a tumbler of scotch or at least
a joint. Then, after a few questions we'd discover that the
woman was taking care of her grandchildren because her
daughter was doing drugs. But the daughter also had the foresight to grab the AFDC checks, and the Department of Public
Aid bureaucrats refused to divert the money from daughter to
granny. Her son was in the County Jail awaiting trial on
"trumped up" charges. The recently purchased couch, because of interest and carrying charges, cost three times what
the merchant sold it for, which was about three times what
any suburbanite would pay for the same furniture—assuming
that anyone would want the garish piece of polyester over
boards sitting in their living room. Besides, the school was
hassling her grandchildren—they were sitting next to her in
front of your desk at 10 a.m. on a school day, eating potato
chips and Twinkies and sipping a Pepsi. Where did you
begin?

The larger frustration was not the inability to resolve
problems, but what happened when you did? Nothing. At
least not for your client. That wasn't supposed to be. The
Great Society, including Legal Services, would improve the
lot of the poor—indeed, do away with poverty. So most of
the think-tank lawyers stayed away from clients, read sociology books, talked to one another and to academic, foundation
types, and filed class-action lawsuits which didn't much improve the lot of the poor. But being downtown and away from
the poor permitted the lawyers to delude themselves into
thinking they had accomplished something. I know. I won

more than a few of these cases. They made me feel good, even gained me publicity, but they didn't do much for my clients.

The four-person Legal Services office I directed was to be different. We would not avoid clients. We would take their issues and cases as we found them and litigate them not only to legal victory but, hopefully, to a better life for our clients. We would succeed where others had failed by concentrating on abused children and their parents, often the victims of poverty and all that goes with it. These folks had futures. And so I met Bill.

On a windswept, unseasonably cold late October evening in 1960, when most of the country's attention was drawn to Richard Nixon and Jack Kennedy, a church worker at an evangelical mission on Chicago's skid row looked out her rear window at a woman and two small kids foraging through the garbage. The church lady took the trio in and fed them. The woman—thin, leathery, with light brown hair—asked the church worker to care for the kids overnight, explaining that she would return the next day. She said her name was Irene. The boy had bright blond hair and was about five. His sister was about a year old.

But Irene didn't return the next day or the day after or the day after that. Finally the church folks phoned the city social service department. A social worker arrived and brought the children to Juvenile Court. The mom did show up about a week later and was told by the church folks to go to the Juvenile Court. She did not, and she was never heard from again. Years later I asked the boy what he recalled about his pre–Juvenile Court life. Not much. A battered pickup truck, a small house in the country, maybe on or near a farm. Grandparents who visited occasionally and a dad, he thought.

Bill's sister was quickly adopted, but Bill's journey was just beginning. He was given a last name and a birth date that made him two years older than he claimed to be. An IQ test based on that age determined that he was "delayed," so he was shipped off to a school for retarded children in Michigan.

Bill's life in the child welfare bureaucracy is a fine example of some of the worst aspects of the system. In those days too many children saved from abusive, neglectful, or abandoning parents were helped in pretty much the same fashion. Bill was a bit different in that he endured every conceivable type of "assistance," and for longer periods of time.

After six months the director of the Michigan school wrote Bill's social worker in Chicago saying that the child probably wasn't retarded since he was pretty much blind without glasses and the IQ test the authorities had given him probably wasn't valid. As it turned out, Bill had done poorly on the IQ test not because of the glasses but because he couldn't read. What's more, the authorities had based Bill's IQ on an age of seven, disregarding his statements that he was five.

According to Bill, the Michigan institution wasn't so bad; he just didn't like his peers. After three years the staff sent him back to Chicago. He went to a foster home, but after several months the foster mother called the cops on Bill, whom she described as a wild child. He had driven the woman's car into a field, and she demanded that the police charge Bill with stealing her car. They refused but, after taking a good look at her house, reported her as being a pretty bad foster parent. But foster parents were, and are, hard to come by, so the child welfare crowd ignored the police, put another kid in the home, and dumped Bill into a detention center to await placement. Bill was still waiting three years later when I interviewed him in the visitors' room.

Like the facility for the retarded, the detention center wasn't bad as jails go. The staff was fairly decent, but the kids were locked up, shackled when they went to court. Freedom was pretty much the four walls of the dormitory and the day room; the meals were institutional, and TV was the main form of recreation and education. By the time I met Bill, he didn't mind the place: incarceration had become a way of life for him. The rules and limits were laid out, and Bill had learned both how to follow and get around them. Since most of the kids passing through were delinquents, he had also learned about the streets.

He was now a towheaded, chubby kid of fourteen, but he looked closer to eleven when I met him in the late sixties at the detention center. He was my first child client. I represented him in four civil rights lawsuits and through him acquired my first major taste of the child welfare and juvenile justice bureaucracies. His cases—and the cases of other children, John, Mary, Pam, Charles, and many others as well as those of some of their parents, like Peter and Lotty—helped forge my views on how to resolve some of the societal problems causing these kids to be separated from their parents and dumped into a less than kindly state child welfare bureaucracy. Today, almost three decades later, I still represent Bill as the guardian of his meager funds. He even works part-time at the Public Guardian's office.

Using Bill as a named plaintiff, we filed a class-action suit to get abused and neglected children out of the detention center, arguing that it made no sense to house innocent children with delinquents. Ultimately we prevailed, and the court ordered the state's child welfare agency, the Department of Children and Family Services (DCFS), to remove all abused and neglected children from that facility. So the agency sent Bill and many other wards to a state psychiatric facility. It took us a while to figure out what had happened, and by the time we did, a couple of hundred state orphans had been housed in various psychiatric hospitals which had more in common with warehouses than mental health. To the degree that any of these kids needed a shrink, it was by virtue of the fact that they had been housed there.

So we sued the Department of Mental Health and DCFS, with DMH being more or less a friendly defendant because they didn't want the kids anyway. Again we won, and the state was ordered to take the kids out of the facilities. But again we lost, because within a year or two most of the children released from the hospitals, along with a lot of other Illinois children, ended up in institutions quickly set up in Texas by entrepreneurs who recognized there were not enough institutions in Illinois to house these kids.

By the time we sued the state of Illinois over this issue, about six hundred abused and neglected children from Chicago were living in Texas facilities. Again we won—at least that's what the media reported—and the kids were brought back home. We also forced the state to close the maximum-security prison for boys and prevailed in several civil rights suits in which the state was compelled to pay money damages to children. In these cases state agencies had failed spectacularly in their responsibility to care for neglected children. I also argued and won the first sexual discrimination case in the United States Supreme Court on behalf of a father whose children the state had taken from him when his common-law wife died.

I left Legal Services and wrote a book about how these cases had reformed our child welfare system. I became a Fellow in a fancy think tank and received a generous, mostly tax-free stipend. Aside from thinking, I met once a month with a couple of dozen other Fellows, most of them writers, former politicians, diplomats, and journalists. Sitting around a large oak table in a Frank Lloyd Wright mansion, we batted about the crises of the day over great food and expensive French wine. My taste in wine would never be the same, but I walked away from the experience with more than that. Throughout my grammar school days, one nun or another would from time to time bellow in frustration, "Patrick Murphy, you aren't thinking!" My think-tank experience corroborated these good women. I wasn't much for sitting around thinking. The fellowship was to last a year, but after four months I resigned and took honest, albeit lower-paying, taxable employment.

I walked away feeling that the shakers and movers, the best and brightest, are overrated at best and phonies at worst. I admit that a study of twenty or so geniuses may not be the best control group, but the cross section was adequate. Several had won Pulitzers; one was a former secretary general of the United Nations; several held high diplomatic posts for our government as well as for foreign ones; two had been governors of our larger states, and several had written best-selling books. About half the crowd were arrogant nincompoops. Some of the others were pretty decent, particularly after we had gone through a case of red wine. Several, like former governor of California Pat Brown, Murray Kempton, a New York journalist, and Neil Sheehan of the *New York Times*, were the kinds of guys who would fit right in at the neighborhood bar. But in truth, the mountain of highfalutin syntax tossed about the table was pretty insubstantial. Indeed, the fellows at the local pub had as much or better insight using simple, monosyllabic Anglo-Saxon words and adjectives rarely heard around the Frank Lloyd Wright table.

About this time Bill was poised to celebrate his twenty-first birthday. The agency responsible for his care, DCFS, had scarcely been meeting its statutory mandate to provide Bill the type of home a good parent should. When not a guest at a prison or psychiatric facility, Bill lived in cheap hotels, on the streets, in abandoned warehouses, and, when he didn't mind the sermon and the guy next to him snoring in his ear, the Pacific Garden Mission. I went back to court and successfully proved that the state had originally given him an erroneous age. The judge lowered his age by three years and ordered DCFS to provide him with the rehabilitative services for which he was now qualified.

At times I dream of all the money I could have made had I pulled out of the juvenile justice field then and devoted my time to reducing people's ages. Instead of spending on psychiatrists and plastic surgeons what would support a poor family for several years, neurotic women would flock to my office and give me the money instead. And all those aging Lotharios wearing shirts open to their navels, romancing twenty-five-year-old bimbos at singles bars, could pay me instead of supporting new wives younger than their daughters.

In any event, winning Bill three more years of state largesse didn't have much of an impact, even though the state treated him better. He received thousands of dollars in therapy and for a while enjoyed a one-on-one social worker and a pretty decent place to stay. The state even bought him a clunker that was as good, even better, than most of the cars he continued to steal.

By the time Bill turned twenty-one for the second time, I was in private practice making a fairly satisfactory living. I represented clients who could afford to pay me and still have enough money to put their lives, or the lives of their loved ones, back together after the mishap that brought them to an unfortunate encounter with our justice bureaucracy. In truth I probably would have forgotten about Bill, in whom I had invested, with various degrees of failure, portions of half a dozen years. But he kept calling and stopping by, preying on my guilt by pointing out, "Patrick, you're all I got . . . I need five bucks." Or, "I'm in the lock up. It's a fucking mistake. Last time, yeah. Not this time."

Until he reached twenty-one Bill had at least a tenuous connection to the Department of Children and Family Services. They were to provide him with services and money and/or a roof. Frequently they were less than a kindly parent, but a goading phone call or the threat of a lawsuit would bring them in line for a while. Even on those many occasions when Bill rejected the safe harbor of state help, he knew it was there. Indeed, the years of institutionalization and incarceration had conditioned him to expect it.

Bill was, still is, an overgrown child. He's not retarded, but he's not quite average either. Whatever happened before skid row, magnified by what occurred afterward, had left him at age twenty-one a young man with massive gaps in his emotions and intellect. As the shrinks say—and did say in his case—he had no superego. Or, as the nuns would have it, no sense of guilt, no real conscience. No sense of right and wrong. Little ability to survive in our late-twentieth-century world. And he's not exactly a master criminal, not even a good thief. He steals from just about anyone. He's stolen from my employees. He even stole from me until I began watching him closely.

But mostly he has stolen cars. I use the present perfect rather than the present tense perhaps optimistically. Sometimes I think he just wants to get caught, like the time he stole a car and drove it in front of a local precinct station, parked it illegally, and stayed in it until he was arrested. Other times, well, he's just not real clever. As when he stole a car and parked it in front of the welfare hotel where he was staying. He happened to look out the window and noticed someone trying to steal his stolen car, whereupon he immediately dialed 911 to report the attempted theft going on beneath his window. He was beside himself with self-righteous rage when I visited him in the lockup a few hours later: "Fuckin' cops. No wonder there's so much crime in this town."

Bill once phoned me from the lockup at Chicago's police headquarters. Another car theft. Would I rescue him? Bill always stole older vehicles because they were easier to get into. Besides, I think instinctively he knew that if he were caught, the punishment would not be as harsh. I spoke to the assistant state's attorney, a young man probably working sixteen hours a day trying cases and writing appeals so he could impress his superiors and get out of misdemeanor courts and into the criminal trial felony courts. I employed my usual Bill shtick. "The kid's a bit loony, not dangerous. Forget his arrest record and convictions. He's had a tough life."

But the prosecutor wasn't listening. "Three years probation on a felony conviction and he walks," he spat from the corner of his mouth, as young prosecutors are wont to do.

"We'll take County Jail time on a misdemeanor."

"No go. We won't reduce."

Further pleas had no effect, so I walked back to the lockup to break the news to Bill that his case would be held over to the felony courts. "For a fuckin' '66 Chevelle?" Bill looked at me in disbelief.

"The state's attorney wants felony probation."

"I walk today?"

"That's right."

"Take it, Patrick. I need it now."

"No go," I replied.

"You'll keep me in this stinking hole when I can walk out right now?"

I explained to Bill why he had to stay in the can rather than enjoy the luxury of the Pacific Garden Mission or whatever halfway house he may have been staying at. Because of his not immodest arrest record at a relatively young age, the state had opted to charge Bill with a felony, a not unusual tactic. The state overcharges in order to force the defendant to settle for a plea on a lesser charge or on probation for a felony charge. The young assistant prosecutor wanted probation on the felony because the felony conviction in a court devoted primarily to misdemeanors would make his record look good. I wanted jail time because Bill couldn't handle probation. If he blew it, as he most certainly would, he'd end up in the penitentiary, which would most certainly kill him. But if we refused the plea bargaining and if the prosecutor wouldn't reduce, the case might be remanded to the felony courts for trial. That meant the Criminal Court building. Here in the misdemeanor court, Bill was not exactly a big fish, but at least he was a medium-sized one among the whores, gamblers, jackrollers, and guys who were caught urinating on State Street. In Criminal Court, the guy who steals an eleven-year-old car is the tiniest of minnows, an irritating little fish to a state's attorney interested in prosecuting the sharks who are the killers, rapists, and armed robbers on his docket. So in Criminal Court, Bill might be able to get a better deal.

I tried to explain to Bill that he couldn't handle probation. But he had a different take. "Patrick, I'm a changed man. I've found Jesus. No more life of crime for me. Get me out. Besides, I got a girlfriend. I got me some steady sex for the first time in my life."

I'm the last person in the world to deprive another man, or woman, of what I prize so much and what is also considered to be one of life's few free pleasures—even if it's really never free. But I tried to explain to Bill how the felony would in the long run deprive him of sex, at least the male/female variety, for a long time, maybe forever, since I was convinced he could never survive the penitentiary.

But Bill wasn't, still isn't, much into deferred gratification. He persisted in standing on his right to plead guilty to the felony.

Now the best word to describe a lawyer is that he or she is a "mouthpiece." A lawyer is supposed to argue—professionally, ethically, and, depending on the circumstances, eloquently—his or her client's case. But a lawyer is also a counselor. A major part of what we do is to advise clients who are unschooled or ignorant of the law and its consequences what could happen to them, given the realities of the case and the precedents of the law. The good lawyer carefully, gently leads the client to what the attorney perceives to be a prudent course of conduct.

I have had more than a few encounters with lawyers who represent children—child advocates they call themselves. Many argue that they must articulate and advocate the child's point of view, no matter how ridiculous or silly. We don't give a seven-year-old the right to vote, a twelve-year-old the right to drive, a fourteen-year-old the right to buy liquor. For good reason: kids are not small adults. They're different. They have less experience, and their sense of time and space is—well, it's kid time and space. If I were to give my kids their choice at dinner every night, it would be simple. Skip the peas and carrots and get right to the hot fudge.

In the Public Guardian's office we take the point of view (and the Illinois courts have confirmed this) that our very difficult job is to advocate what is in the child's best interest, while informing the court when the child's wishes deviate from what we pursue. This is unquestionably true with a young child. As the child grows into adolescence, the pendulum swings toward our role as a mouthpiece in appropriate cases, while in other cases best interest still predominates.

My major complaint with child advocates is their willingness naively to propose even the silliest adolescent notion of their clients without ever employing their role as counselor. I've had thousands of clients, many of them children and adolescents, and not once at the end of a "counseling" session have I had any of them disagree with me. Even headstrong, all-adults-are-stupid teenagers become sober when a lawyer looks them in the eye and explains the facts and consequences of a course of conduct.

But Bill wasn't a child, chronologically. He looked me in the eye and said, "Fuck you, Patrick. I want the probation."

Sometimes there are exceptions to careful, gentle lawyerly counseling, leading a client to your point of view. The turnkey didn't look up from the sports section as I heaved Bill against the wall. As he was trying to regroup, I grabbed his shirt, flung him around, put my face a couple of inches from his, and shouted, "I don't give a flying fuck what you think. You're not copping out." I let him crumple to the floor and stormed out to the courtroom where sleeping cops sprawled in front-row benches and pimps waited for their prostitutes' cases to be called and dismissed.

Twenty minutes later the sheriff brought Bill out. The state's attorney informed the judge that we had rejected a reasonable plea offer and he had no choice but to remand the case to Criminal Court for felony prosecution. The judge, with fifty other cases on his call, was perfectly happy to get rid of this one and was signing the order when he noticed Bill growling at me and acting more than a little agitated. "Is something wrong?"

"No, your honor," I said.

"Is that correct?" the judge asked, looking at Bill.

"Something is very wrong," Bill replied in a loud, raspy voice that reverberated throughout the courtroom. "For the first time in my life I'm getting steady pussy and Patrick wants me to stay in jail. I want probation. I want to cop out. I stole the fuckin' car."

You could hear a pin drop in the courtroom as the judge looked from Bill to me and back at Bill again. When his gaze fell upon me, I could see he was trying to determine who was crazier, the client or the mouthpiece. "Mr. Defendant," he said, "follow your lawyer's advice."

Several months without his girlfriend later, Bill walked out of jail with time served. A couple of months later he married the young woman he was seeing steadily. The judge who lowered his age officiated, and I was the best man. They were an odd couple in some ways but made for each other. Janice, an African American, was both mentally and physically impaired. The physical problems mostly, but also her years in various state psychiatric facilities, had left her as mean as a junkyard dog. Throughout their fifteen years together she and Bill had monumental fights, some of which put one or both of them in jail for a night. Her death devastated Bill in a way I couldn't have anticipated, since I had always felt he was incapable of deep feelings. But a year or so later he married another mentally impaired woman, also black, but a much more pleasant person than his first wife.

After Bill turned twenty-one I did sue DCFS on his behalf and several years later settled for $100,000. We eked maybe ten years out of the money and bought him a used car which he tore apart while he continued to steal other vehicles. My greatest legal victories have probably been the series of losses involving Bill's many stolen cars. We lost the battles but won the war. Bill did a lot of County Jail time, and some in psychiatric institutions, but no penitentiary time. He could never have survived that.

Now Bill and his second wife live in a dingy couple of rooms in a hotel filled with welfare recipients. They survive on Social Security disability and the few bucks he earns working part-time for our office, cleaning the apartments and homes of our elderly wards. Along the way he has fathered three kids, one by his first wife and two by his present one. He and wife number one did have custody of the first child for about six months before I realized the situation was hopeless and called DCFS, who ultimately took the child. I also felt compelled to report the birth of his additional children. I like Bill. His second wife is okay. But they are little more than children themselves, and certainly incapable of *raising* children.

When I first met Bill and began to sue state and county officials over his plight and that of other children, I don't think I was arrogant enough to believe that a lawsuit would make Bill a commodities broker or force the child welfare bureaucracy to become a decent parent. But I probably thought we would make life much better for Bill and the other DCFS urchins. In fact, we failed.

But not entirely, or I wouldn't still be in the business and wouldn't be writing this. Bill's life is marginally better than if we had never represented him. True, we put in a lot of time, effort, and taxpayers' money for a millimeter of progress, but progress for those who are so far gone can only be measured in millimeters. What the state of Illinois did to Bill wasn't pretty, but the state didn't ask for Bill and it didn't create him. His first five or six years left him a very messed up kid and set the stage for a very messed up life. The point is that even good state agency care, if there can be such an animal, is no substitute for a decent parent.

The benefit for those of us who work in the trenches is that we keep in touch with humanity. Like my dinner with Bill at a restaurant in Michigan in January 1995. We had driven a rental truck from Chicago and were about to stay at a home I owned in Michigan, where we would move furniture the next day. The waitress taking our orders eyed us like we didn't belong, at least together.

Outside of a courtroom I'm a relatively soft-spoken guy, despite my South Side Chicago roots and hard edges. Bill is about five feet eight inches, chunky, blond, with bright blue eyes behind thick glasses. He's about forty, though he looks younger. His clothes, whose odor might offend some, look like they're off the Salvation Army rack, though in truth at least some are my castoffs. His voice is loud, his sentences ungrammatical, often non sequiturs. At the time he wore a three-day stubble. I suspect he comes across like someone who has spent the better part of his life in prisons and mental-health facilities.

I remember this commonplace dinner in Michigan because I felt connected. I've never had the experience of a power lunch, dinner, or breakfast, or even a power meeting, and I have no regrets. I'll take my power-free dinner with Bill anytime.

3

PRESERVING FAMILIES, KILLING CHILDREN

In July and August, Chicago's weather is not unlike Mogadishu's, except that Somalia's humidity and heat don't come with pollution. On one of those sludgy, oppressively hot August days when I was sweating dirt, I got a call from an animal control expert—dogcatcher we called them when I was a kid. "Walter here. You're the man. I've seen you on TV. You probably seen me rescuing that dog from the Chicago River last spring. I got on most of the channels. Got a hot one here. Need you pronto. Yesterday."

I explained to Walter that the Public Guardian represented children, not animals. But he was not to be put off, and several hours later he exploded into my office. Mid-fifties, with horn-rimmed glasses perched crookedly on a beaklike nose, Walter was a mass of energy, one of those rare guys who loves his job even after spending the better part of a lifetime at it. He told tales of many years of saving animals and, on occasion, people—mostly children—from animals gone bad. He was an animal control superstar. He pulled commendations from a file and spoke of the cruelty that dumb animals suffer at the hands of even dumber ones, us. I tried to get him to the point.

"I've seen worse, mind you. But this was a beaut. Jones from Human Resources phoned me last week. She got complaints about a foul stench from a flat over a tavern at Grand and Ashland. No way she'd go in alone 'cause of the dogs, so she called me. Called DCFS too, because the neighbors said a kid was there.

"So we get the cops and go for it. Christ. I thought I was in a time warp. I dealt with this family twelve, maybe thirteen years ago." He opened one of several accordion folders he carried with him, handing me a crumpled newspaper article from 1981.

The parents, Edward P. Lisokowski, 53, and his wife, Josephine, 39, were arrested Tuesday and charged with child neglect by endangering the life and health of a child. Two children, Edwardine, 5, and Joseph, 4, were taken from the home by the Department of Children and Family Services.

The couple's youngest child, Mary, six weeks, was taken to Cook County Hospital on April 21, suffering from tetanus. Police said the infection apparently developed when Mrs. Lisokowski severed the child's umbilical cord after giving birth in the couple's home.

Detective Sordo said one of the couple's children died about a year ago, apparently from a similar infection after the umbilical cord was cut by the mother.

Police said the odor in the "animal house" was overpowering and that animal and fur droppings covered the floors.

Animal Control Inspector Walter Kale told the judge he had removed, among other things, fifteen dogs, a rabbit, a duck, a myna bird, a finch, a hamster, a gerbil, four pigeons, a parrot and a large turtle from the home, along with two dead parakeets.

Other animals remain, Kale said, but there was so much garbage and debris in six vacant apartments in the building that the animals could build tunnels and hide in them.

Walter told me that DCFS had removed another child from the Lisokowski home in 1974 under similar circumstances. Ultimately the city tore down the Lisokowskis' home in 1981 because it was beyond repair.

He took the clipping back and, carefully folding it, placed it in his portable file. "The joint over the tavern was just as sick as the other two. They had sealed the windows. The place was hot like a jungle but with a steamy awful stench. Shit and piss everywhere, human and animal. Twenty or so dogs yelping, howling, barking, and running all over the place. Shit in the twelve-year-old kid's hair, on his clothes. The old man, the husband, lying in a corner covered with shit, his leg black with gangrene. I got the dogs out of there pronto, poor miserable animals. The Human Resources lady got the old man and kid to the hospital. The aides took a couple of hours just to clean him up."

"And the kid?" I asked.

"After the hospital cleaned him up, DCFS took him back to his mom. Jones and I and the cops told the worker that if these people couldn't take care of dogs, how they gonna care for the kid? But the worker said all mom needs is some parenting classes, a homemaker, and she'll be okay."

We have had other animal/family preservation cases. Like the retarded woman with the six-month-old failure-to-thrive child. The doctors insisted that the woman was incapable of mothering. Social workers argued that a homemaker and intensive casework services already in place for several months needed more time to kick in. But the physicians took the case to court, where DCFS's own records revealed that the lady's flat was "filthy, has stench, has many animals in home, i.e., guinea pig [large], several dogs, cats, a litter of cats, a monkey."

The judge left the monkey but did remove the child.

The Adoption Assistance Act of 1980, as strengthened in 1993, mandates that states must use reasonable efforts to prevent foster care placements. Once a child is placed in foster care, states must make every effort to return the child to his family as quickly as possible. The act requires "permanency planning" once a child is in foster care. Although adoption is an alternative, permanency planning has been interpreted by child welfare agencies to mean that all efforts must be directed at returning children to their original homes.

Family preservation is thus a philosophy that translates into specific programs. The philosophy is that children should remain at home or be returned to home as soon as possible. The various family preservation programs spawned in at least thirty-five states provide that a family that abuses or neglects a child is entitled to intensive services for periods of six to twelve weeks. These services include intensive social work, parenting classes, a homemaker in the home for up to five days a week, deposits and even rent payments for new apartments, a psychiatrist, chauffeuring services, bus fare, baby-sitting, and cash money.

The rationale behind these programs is that most abusive parents are as much a victim as their child—though not by a much larger and stronger person. The parents are victimized by poverty, racism, unemployment, discrimination, domestic violence, sexism, and half a dozen other isms. Family preservation advocates do not dismiss the violence that these misguided parents visit upon their defenseless children; they argue rather that the kids need their parents, and besides, our system of substitute care isn't exactly wonderful. In the 1970s, as a practicing attorney, I vigorously advocated family preservation, in part because of cases like Lotty Irvin's.

In the late seventies Lotty Irvin phoned. Would I visit her? Would she come down to my office? I countered. Don't get out much. Couldn't I come by? she pleaded. So I did. In those relatively innocent days, white people ventured into the heart of Chicago's West Side alone and unarmed. It still happens, but now middle-class people of any race more often encounter hostility and danger in underclass neighborhoods. Of course the majority of the underclass who live there are decent, law-abiding folks who live with danger and hostility every day.

The other day I went to a wake I'd just as soon have avoided. I have known the mother for twenty years. She is a wonderful woman who used to work for me. The father is a lawyer, a good guy who devotes his free time to coaching local grammar school basketball teams. The family lives in Lincoln Park, one of the city's swankier neighborhoods. The murder was the lead on the evening news and a front-page story. The death was every parent's nightmare. The young man, twenty-one years old and a college junior, went to a party with friends. Four young thugs held him up as he parked his car behind his folks' home. He tried reasoning with his assailants but ended up with five bullets in his back and dying in his father's arms. How do parents survive such a death? They don't in any real sense.

Lotty lost a child too, a three-month-old. That was in 1973. It didn't make the news, not even the obits. But she suffered just as much as my friends. I don't know where Lotty is today. Someone told me she was dead. I can believe it. The last time I saw her, the time I drove out to the West Side, she looked okay, but emotionally she was a wreck. It happens that way in the ghetto. One day a woman with a few kids and no involved dad is surviving. Her kids are okay. Then something happens—a son gets in trouble, a lover walks out, a fire, a nasty welfare bureaucrat. Maybe just a rat in the house or, as in Lotty's case, a dead infant.

Wasted

Her flat was up a couple of flights of stairs in a three-story crumbling brick affair that didn't stand out in a neighborhood of similar buildings near shuttered factories. In less than a century the neighborhood had seen waves of Germans, Irish, Italians, Jews, Poles, and blacks hoping to escape tyranny and poverty, only to be confronted by exploitation and ultimately conformity. These buildings had witnessed battles for gain, fights from frustration, booze from failure, and brutality from poverty.

Lotty's wooden door was protected by a metal, padlocked gate. She opened it and let me into a neat, Spartanly furnished room. She was thinner than when I had last seen her. But she still had strong features, dark shiny skin, and a sensuous presence. She handed me a Coke, sat opposite, and stared at me a long time without speaking. I looked past her out grey windows at vacant lots and burned-out hulks of buildings. I prattled small talk. Where were her sons? Noplace. Nowhere, she responded. How was she doing? Not bad. Okay, she mumbled.

In 1970, shortly after her third child was born, her husband had walked out. Within a year she fell under the spell of one of the various welfare reformers working the West Side. She and several other welfare mothers moved into an abandoned church claiming that adequate alternative housing was unavailable. The owners ignored the women, who remained for a couple of years. But then developers bought the church and wanted to demolish it. They were reasonable and gave the families time to move out. By December 1972 only Lotty and her now four kids remained.

In the late night hours of December 17, four cops showed

up at Lotty's door. They said they had received complaints from the welfare folks that she had not fed her children properly. No doubt the developers were using the police to do their dirty work. The officers ransacked the cupboards and said there wasn't enough food. The kids would have to go down to the station. They'd have to call DCFS. Lotty went after one of the cops, which wasn't very smart since they were bigger, there were more of them, and they were certainly better armed. Besides, assaulting a police officer is a felony. They wrestled her to the floor, cuffed her, and transported her to the County Jail. The kids went to three different foster homes, the oldest boy and the youngest girl, three months, into the same one.

A week or so later some nuns bailed Lotty out. When the church people, Lotty, and some of her welfare friends tried to find her kids, they discovered they were in foster care. Several days later a DCFS social worker contacted the nun and told her to inform Lotty (who didn't have a phone) that the three-month-old had been accidentally killed in a foster home. Apparently a not too bright adolescent foster child had dropped the baby into a bathtub of scalding water.

Once Lotty was a strong, militant woman, but when I met her in January 1973 she was subdued, compliant, and willing to go along with whatever DCFS said. She didn't question why her kids were in foster care or how or why her daughter had died. She pleaded with me to help get her son out of the same foster home in which her baby had been killed.

I did. I also arranged to have her other three sons returned to her and successfully represented her in the criminal trial. When she phoned, I hadn't seen her in five or six years.

The woman sitting in front of the dingy windows and just a few years older than me, about forty, was completely beaten and not entirely with it.

I wish I could repeat what she said, even paraphrase it. I think she spoke of "the Good Lawd," and his "good plan" for all the "good peoples, black and white," and "peoples like me and you, Mr. Murphy, we is heaven bound." And I think she spoke about rats and roaches and the stench and black boys, and she did refer to pimps and black girls giving sex to old men. She may have spoken about girls having babies too young and nursing them on pop, and even about most white folks in the ghetto being "johns and dopers looking for sex and drugs."

She also spoke about her baby—what she would be like if she were still alive, what she would be like if she grew up in the ghetto. Maybe she was better off with "the good Lawd" before she had a chance to really live.

Not long after I represented Lotty in 1973, I wrote a book in which I pleaded for programs to keep families together. I advocated the same approach on three occasions when I testified before congressional committees. I used Lotty's case and the cases of others I had represented as examples of why family preservation programs would be better for children and certainly cheaper for the taxpayers. Congress took my advice and that of thousands of other lawyers, judges, and social workers, and in 1980 passed the Adoption Assistance Act, mandating family preservation and family reunification.

In November 1978 I received a call from the governor of Illinois, Jim Thompson. I had gotten to know Jim when I was a young prosecutor and he had just left the state's attorney's office and was teaching at Northwestern University Law School. We shared a few drinks and war stories, but over the years we went our divergent ways. I went to frustration in Somalia and "victories" with Bill, Lotty, and others. Thompson, as a federal prosecutor, gained a national reputation putting famous Illinois politicians in federal country club prisons. He parlayed his fame into the governor's mansion. Shortly after he became governor, he called. The local CBS affiliate had been lambasting him because of an obscure official, the Cook County Public Guardian. He asked me to take over the office for three months, clean it up, and issue a report. I told him I had never heard of the office. A silence followed and then a laugh. "Neither have I. Do me a favor and take the damn thing over."

So on a part-time basis I did. The Public Guardian was then a weird lady with pink hair who was either a crook or pretty negligent. The office took care of disabled elderly people who had estates and no one to look after them. Personal items had disappeared from the wards' estates, and all but one of the Public Guardian's charges were stuck in nursing homes or psychiatric hospitals. In any event, one thing led to another, and I remained Public Guardian part-time.

We suggested that the office become truly a county office, appointed by the chief judge of the Circuit Court. One of the first things I did was to sue the Department of Mental Health and the governor over the conditions in one of the psychiatric facilities in which some of our wards had been placed. It never dawned on me that Thompson might get angry because I sued him. He did, but at least he didn't fire me. That act, however, and a few dozen others, was probably the genesis of my reputation as something less than a team player.

In 1986 the local Legal Services office sued the chief judge over the Guardian's office at the Juvenile Court. The lawyers who worked for the office were supposed to represent abused children. Instead most had private practices and considered the kids a nuisance. The chief judge asked me to investigate and report back to him. To make a long and some would say an immodest story short, I filed a report suggesting that the judge terminate the chief attorney in the office, a good man who had let himself be bullied by clouted politicians. I suggested he appoint a tough, no-nonsense fellow—me. The chief judge accepted my advice, and I gave up my private practice and went full-time as Public Guardian. (We now have in our office about 150 lawyers and 75 other professionals, including social workers, investigators, and paralegals, providing guardianship services to the elderly disabled and legal services to abused children as well as some kids in divorce cases. We are the largest office of its kind in the world—primarily because we are the *only* such office.)

Except for an occasional foray to represent a parent or a delinquent kid for a fee, or a neglected child pro bono, I had been away from Juvenile Court for nearly a dozen years. The gritty grey building was gone, replaced by one that was large, ugly, and rust colored. (In 1994 an addition, as large as the original, was added and became obsolete as soon as it was built.)

I expected to find DCFS screwing up kids' lives as they

had in the sixties and seventies. They were. And when they do, it makes good press—and better lawsuits. But in truth, public child welfare agencies will never be satisfactory. We give them children whose spirits have been crushed by oafish parents and expect the agency to put the kids' psyches back together. In most cases they don't. In some cases they make the kids worse.

But I also expected that by the mid-eighties family preservation would have made a difference, that a lot more kids would be staying home. I was right on both counts. Family preservation had made a major difference, and the kids were staying home. But the difference was not an improvement.

Gradually over the next several years my views on family preservation and reunification changed. Preserving families is a good idea in a "proper" case, but such cases are unfortunately not as common as they used to be. And Father Flanagan's dictum about "no such thing as a bad boy" has been modified by many child welfare workers into "no parents are bad parents." But the kids and parents coming into the big-city courts are different from a generation ago. The files I kept seeing and the cases I kept trying, and those the lawyers I supervise brought to my attention, altered my view.

Siaonia was one of six children whom DCFS admitted died over a three-year period, while their families were being preserved. In December her aunt called the DCFS hot line to report that her sister and her sister's boyfriend had been beating two-and-a-half-year-old Siaonia, who weighed seventeen pounds. DCFS assigned an agency to work on preserving the family. I'll let their notes tell the story:

12/4   Worker made initial visit to client home. Worker explained the allegations to the client. Client reported that the child had fallen from her bunkbed. The client's house appeared nice and clean. Worker explained the Family First program to the client. Client discussed her family background and she [sic] that she lived with parmore [sic], [mother's boyfriend].

12/9   Client was attending parenting class. Paramour was caring for the children. Worker noticed that the two year and [sic] scratches on her back. This worker chose not to question paramour but will question mother at the next home visit. . . .

1/13   Worker transported client to Ford City Shopping Center to assist client in looking for shoes for her son. Worker and client ate lunch while discussing client's new job and the disagreement between paranour [sic] and MGM.

1/14   Worker, homemaker and client went to Lincoln Mall. This is to get the mother out of the house for the day. The home and children were going on as usual.

1/17   Homemaker made home visit. Homemaker was there to support client and to assist in household management. Workers met with mother and children. The home was neat and clean and the children appeared well kept. Worker informed homeaker [sic] that she will be visiting this family in about two weeks. . . .

2/17 Worker and homemaker took client out for dinner. This would be the last visit for the homemaker. Client discussed her wedding plans. Siaonia is gaining weight. . . .

3/17 [Mother's] children range from 8 months old to 4 years old. Currently, [paramour] is the second caretaker in the home. [Mother] and her three children reside in a well furnished, two bedroom, apartment, in Altgeld Gardens. They have two colored television sets and all new appliances. [Mother] appears to manage her income from public aid well. The children are always well dressed and the [sic] is plenty of food in the home. [Mother] utilizes the community resources that are available to her; i.e. the clinic in Altgeld Gardens, the WIC program and the Department of Human Services. . . .

[Mother] appears to be a very introverted individual. She is not very easy going and attempts to please only her paramour and his family. Due to the presence of a homemaker, the amount of stress and frustration has been reduced. [Mother] appears to have a lot more patience with her children and she continues to improve her disciplinary techniques. . . .

Since the involvement of the Family First Unit workers, this family has received a homemaker from Family Care Services who has been working with [Mother] on appropriate disciplinary skills. This family also received funds for Chritmas [sic] toys, winter supplies and a chest of drawers for the baby.

This worker recommends the case of [Mother] be

closed with the Department of Children and Family Services based on the following:

1.) Mother has complied with the Family Preservation Program.

2.) Due to the services provided, this family has become stabilized.

3.) Mother will continue to utilize community services for emergency [sic] food, milk and clothing.

3/17 Mother called client crying and stating she was at the hospital and that her child had fell [sic] in the bathtub and died. Worker told client that she would meet her at her home. Client stated that the police were holding her there and that they have alleged that she had killed her child. . . .

The mother's sister had phoned in the original abuse report in December that prompted the family preservation services. On February 22 she again phoned the child abuse hot line, reporting that Siaonia had burn marks on her wrist and back and a bite mark on her back. But, apparently satisfied with mom's rehabilitation, the agency did nothing.

On March 17 Siaonia was brought into the hospital DOA. After offering various stories to the police, the mother confessed that "The baby had wet herself and she wanted to clean her. The baby was sitting on the side of the tub and the boiling water was next to the tub. She [Mother] leaned the baby over backwards and poured the boiling water on her groin area. The baby started to cry and she turned her over and poured water on her buttocks. . . ." In fact the skin in and around the girl's vagina and anus had been completely scalded off. For good measure, her head was bashed in. But there was more. According to hospital notes, the visible injuries were:

Ligature marks to both wrists;
Ligature marks to both ankles;
Fresh scratches to left cheek;
Fresh scratches to right side of neck;
Fresh scratches to left side of neck;
Bruised left eye;
Bruised right eye;
Discolored and bruised forehead;
Severe fresh burn to right of navel;
Severe fresh burn to vaginal area, skin peeling;
Severe fresh burn to buttocks, skin peeling;
Multiple bruises to the back;
Multiple bruises to the chest;
Multiple bruises to the arms;
Puncture wound to right heel.

The final autopsy report chronicled more than forty separate bruises and burns on Siaonia's body, most incurred while the social worker and homemaker were visiting their "client."

The child welfare system has failed children because it refuses to distinguish between parents who are ill-equipped to raise their children adequately without help, and parents who are too immature or thuggish to raise children even with help. To the system, all parents are victims, irrespective of their crimes or potential for reform. And the parent, not the child, is the client. In Siaonia's case, for example, the notes repeatedly referred to the client as the mother, seldom mentioning Siaonia.

Thirty-year-old Patricia had seven kids between seven months and thirteen years of age. On a half-dozen occasions, child welfare workers investigated, cited, and charged her with child neglect. Finally they gave her a homemaker. According to the child welfare worker, "The family has come a long way since I began working with them. . . ." And his notes showed, " . . . A homemaker . . . has been involved with the . . . family for approximately ten months. Her help has been invaluable. She is in the home for 16 hours a week. She has done such things as accompany [Patricia] to clothing, furniture, grocery stores, etc. She has babysit for [Patricia] when she has scheduled appropriate appointments. She has helped [Patricia] in her daily routine around her apartment, budgeting, food preparation, chores, and the gentle coordinating of children activities."

Shortly after that report was completed, Patricia's eleven-year-old daughter, Denise, ran to a neighbor pleading for help. The neighbor called the police. Later Chicago Police Officer Schultz reported:

> Upon inspection of the premises, it was observed that the living conditions were deplorable. There was no electricity, running water or food in the residence. The toilet was backed up and there was human feces on the floor. . . . Observed six other children of Patricia . . . in a state of complete and total neglect; no food, no clothes, no gas or

electricity; these children ranging in age from five years to nine months.

Officer Ann Alvear later testified about the

... smell, the first thing you noticed was the smell of urine and feces. . . . The entire apartment was littered with glass, broken bottles and beer cans. Basically we had to kick our way through the apartment, through the garbage. Officer Alvear went on to point out that she found two infants in soiled diapers on a cot with bottles of curdled milk nearby, and she found two naked boys and naked three year old girl. When we walked in, she ran up and grabbed me and she wouldn't let me go. . . . And she was filthy. She had bugs in her hair; there was stuff jumping out of her hair . . . rancid food and roaches. The bathroom floor had been used as a toilet and there did not appear to be running water.

At the later trial, Peggy O'Connor, an eighteen-year veteran of the Chicago Police Department, relayed the ordeal of Patricia's daughter Denise. The mother had ordered her eleven-year-old to "lay on a mattress beside her" with a man. "The man told Patricia . . . that he wanted to have sex with Denise. Denise started crying and told her mother she didn't want to do it. Patricia told Denise that she had to do it. The man then attempted to insert his penis in Denise's vagina. This activity took place for approximately five minutes." Later he stuck his finger into her vagina. Then the man "put his penis in the mouth of the eleven year old child after she had begged her mother, Patricia, to make it stop happening.

And Patricia White told her daughter to open her mouth."
The policewoman testified that Patricia told Denise she
would kill her if she told anyone. In exchange for pimping her
eleven-year-old daughter, Patricia White received some
karachi, "which is a liquid form of heroin and the promise of
cocaine, fifty dollars United States currency and a pair of ten-
nis shoes."

The infusion of intensive one-on-one services is the key component in most family preservation programs. A social
worker, a homemaker, and six weeks to three months later—
presto! a developmentally delayed or schizophrenic or crack-
addicted parent suffering a reality-based depression caused
by three kids, no education, no job, and no involved father (in
many cases all of the above) will be cured and ready for responsible parenthood.

Guilt and responsibility, pillars of the criminal justice
system, are alien concepts in the juvenile justice arena. Instead the child welfare industry and the juvenile courts consider only a child's best interest, which is often honored in
their breach. The parent's abusive acts become irrelevant
once the Juvenile Court determines that a child has been
abused. Instead the courts and the child welfare bureaucracy
are responsible for providing services to the parent(s).

Federal and most state laws mandate that the bureaucracies must employ reasonable efforts to rehabilitate the parents. Since state child welfare agencies frequently do not
operate like a well-oiled machine, they often fail to provide
what courts interpret as "adequate" services for the parent.
As a result, kids stay in the system, floating amongst foster

homes, ultimately becoming unadoptable and living on the streets while the parent may occasionally visit and hold out just enough hope for rehabilitation that the system refuses to terminate parental rights. Because even a marginal parent is better for most kids than a state bureaucracy or a foster home, the state *should* try to rehabilitate the parents in proper cases so that children can go home. But the parents must bear the brunt of the responsibility for reuniting the family. Any decent parent would walk barefoot over a mountain of cut glass to get his child back. I cannot tell you the number of times I have endured lawyers for the parents arguing that he or she did not have the transportation money to visit the child in a different part of town while the parent, about 250 pounds of well-fed girth, stood by nodding affirmatively.

In the present system, the parent's victim status becomes more important than the child's neglect. We questioned the homemaker in Siaonia's case:

> QUESTION: Did [the social worker] tell you what she wanted you to talk to the mother about?
>
> ANSWER: No. She wanted someone to talk to her because she was down and depressed and she just wanted someone to talk to. And me as a mother, they figured she wanted me to go out there to talk to her. . . .
>
> QUESTION: Did [the social worker] tell you anything about abuse or neglect that occurred in the case?
>
> ANSWER: No.
>
> QUESTION: Did she tell you that she wanted you to assess whether abuse had, in fact, occurred in the home?
>
> ANSWER: No. . . .

QUESTION: Did you ask [your supervisors] or anyone else if any of the children in the home had been abused or neglected?

ANSWER: No, I didn't. It wasn't my job just to question them as if they were abused or neglected, something like that.

QUESTION: And nobody told you that either?

ANSWER: No. It wasn't forthcoming.

The homemaker, apparently a decent but unschooled person, was to chat with the mother, make a few meals, take her to the mall, buy her lunch—and three months later mom would be fine, despite being not much more than twenty, with no high school education, three kids fathered by a lout who walked out on her, and a boyfriend sponging off welfare money meant for the kids.

In 1990 twenty-five-year-old Beatrice told her wheelchair-bound mother to look after her young kids, she was going to get the welfare check. Two days later, when Beatrice still hadn't come home, grandma called the state. According to investigators, the six children ". . . were without coats. Poor hygiene . . . standing water . . . soiled pampers throughout bedroom floor. Holes in walls and falling plaster. . . . Older children admitted they had not had any breakfast for two days, only lunch at school and a sandwich for dinner. Infant was saturated with urine when child was taken into protective custody. Worker changed pamper and baby was so raw from diaper rash, skin literally came off in diaper. There was no food at all in the refrigerator, all baby formula was spoiled even bottle child was drinking from. . . ."

The social workers took custody of the children but quickly returned them to their mother. And now, not because of her poverty—after all, just about everyone in her neighborhood was dirt poor—but because of her crack habit, she was a victim entitled to a homemaker five days a week, new beds, and workmen to install a hot water heater and fix the holes in the ceiling and walls. It is unclear what the homemaker did. Some homemakers provide counseling, as in Siaonia's case, others help with chores around the house or are supposed to teach the mother how to nurture a child. This homemaker apparently stayed in the home for close to two years.

Four years and three additional kids later, mom again left without leaving a forwarding address. Grandma again phoned the authorities. The report sounded pretty much like an echo: "Worker found [the children] partially clothed and hungry, living in an unbearable residence. [One child] had diarrhea and when worker changed his diaper he was found to have corroded penis and buttocks." And later: "74 year old maternal grandmother states [mother] left home three days ago and hasn't returned. States she is unable to care for children because she is wheelchair bound. States mother is a drug abuser and neglects her children. The children are not receiving adequate food and clothing. . . . Worker found this residence deplorable, debris and garbage was strewn all over the house, one half inch of water covered the kitchen floor. Maternal grandmother's potty chair was full of fecal material. There was rotten food on the kitchen table. Garbage also covered the kitchen floor. There was no food in the refrigerator or cabinets. The worker found four small children ranging from 1 to 6 years old partially clothed and hungry. . . ."

The child welfare agency's chief spokesperson explained the case away by saying, "From the time we've been involved with the family, we've been dealing with issues related to poverty. . . . We can't take children away just because of poverty, and just about everything here . . . relates to poverty."

Statements like this one turn decent folks into welfare "reformers" who would do away with all safety nets and fuel the arguments of racists. Most very poor folks, most underclass mothers (even those whose boyfriends flee when free sex leads to the possible responsibility of a child) do a good job, don't take crack, don't walk out on their kids, and don't leave their flats to garbage, feces, and rats. Like the rest of us, they want only the best for their children, even if they are often too overwhelmed to provide it. But viewers of the late news don't hear about these responsible poor folks. They see bureaucrats and "advocates" defending or explaining away outrageous behavior that infuriates other poor people as much as the rest of us.

Child welfare workers are relentless in their attempts to reunify the parents with the children, even . . . well, I'll let the *Chicago Tribune* explain it.

A mother who stood idly by as her boyfriend repeatedly sexually and physically abused her three daughters, including one who later died, should be flown at taxpayer expense to Florida four times a year to visit her two surviving girls, Illinois officials are recommending. . . .

At the trial, testimony showed that [the mother] had for years stood idly by as her three daughters were beaten and raped by [the boyfriend]. In some instances, she had been in the same bed with [the boyfriend] as he sexually attacked her daughters, according to testimony.

[The mother] also was implicated in some of the physical abuse of the girls, but never was charged criminally. On the day [the child] suffered her fatal burns, [the mother] went to work instead of taking the girl to the hospital, testified [the mother's] oldest daughter, who was then 10. [The child] was left with her two older sisters, who tried to comfort her as she slowly went into shock and the skin peeled off her body.

Family preservation services have been stupidly lavished on irresponsible and cowardly people who take advantage of a child's vulnerability to harm her or him, then cower behind their poverty to justify their actions. Helping parents like Lotty is still a laudable idea. Kids are better off with even marginal parents than in a system of substitute care that will never be much more than marginal. But those who administer these programs must shoot with a rifle, not a shotgun, to help keep kids with responsible if temporarily overwhelmed parents.

While we need responsible family preservation programs, we must also understand how counterproductive this philosophy can be. Most poor people do a credible job, under bleak circumstances, of raising their children—and receive not one additional penny from the government. Under family preservation, irresponsible behavior is rewarded; responsible behavior is thus denigrated.

Take any floor of any housing project in the nation. Seven or eight families struggle heroically against impossible odds to raise their kids. Three or four do a marginal job, while one or two crack-addicted parents abuse their kids or leave them alone while they go out partying. Which family gets the home-maker, money, intensive social work services, chauffeuring to and from appointments, and several months' rent for a new apartment? You got it. The message to the underclass is, act irresponsibly and get help. Act responsibly and get nothing. Since this patronizing message involves an underclass which in our major cities is chiefly African-American, it is also a racist message, though unintentionally so.

Self-proclaimed compassionate Democrats champion family preservation, but so do no-nonsense, act-responsible Republicans. The left embraces it. The right loves it. Foundation types cherish it.

The left sees the poor as victims who harm their kids for want of a social worker, psychiatrist, and housekeeper. The right dismisses the poor as having made their beds, so let them rot at home without government handouts. And the right recognizes that family preservation costs much less than decent foster homes, group homes, residential care, and psychiatric counseling for children, the real victims of child abuse. Besides, since family preservation became fashionable, children pouring into the Juvenile Court have become increasingly less attractive—fewer blond and blue-eyed, more black and kinky-haired.

The left is as racist in its own patronizing way as it claims the right to be. Not that either is really prejudiced. Compared to when I was a young man, raw racism is way down. But patronizing minorities is a more subtle and in some ways a more insidious form of racism. We expect little of inner-city kids.

Indeed, the hardest part of my job is coming to court in the morning and seeing kids the same age as my own two boys, with the same potential, but whom I know will end up in jail, drop out of school, have kids when they should be reading Edgar Allan Poe, and ultimately become nonproductive broken men and women before they are my age.

Child abuse and neglect issues are highly charged and infinitely complex. In all but a relatively few cases, such as sex abuse, torture, and serious mental impairment, the initial emphasis must be on preserving families, if possible without court intervention. If the court must get involved in order to protect children, they should be returned as quickly as possible to their parents.

There are excellent reasons why this should be the starting point of the discussion. Our state-run substitute-care system leaves too much to be desired. More important, even most abused children have developed bonds with their parents. Removing a child from a parent is neither for amateurs nor the faint of heart. It is complex, major surgery which in most cases will adversely affect the lives of both parents and children.

Children taken from an abusive parent and placed in even an outstanding foster home will at some level miss their parent and probably suffer some emotional trauma. Children taken from a parent and placed in a mediocre foster home, or left to float through a series of foster homes, ending up in institutions, will miss their parents and suffer considerable emotional damage.

The proponents of family preservation correctly press these issues to advance their cause. But there is another side of the coin: the nature of the parents.

The trauma a child will experience in breaking a bond with the parent must be balanced against the trauma the child will experience in remaining *with* a parent, or being returned to a parent who is simply unable to nurture a child or, worse, uses his or her power to destroy the child.

Our business is as imperfect as the human condition. Although social workers, judges, and lawyers in the child welfare and juvenile justice systems continually mouth the words "best interest of the child," in most cases we are incapable of doing what is in the child's best interest. More often we try to accomplish what is not in the child's worst interest.

Our natural inclinations are to sympathize with the parent or parents, particularly those mired in the hopelessness of the underclass. But at some point we must consider the child, particularly since a child's time frame is entirely different from ours. Family preservation has often failed because it has been pushed vigorously by conservatives who see it as a way to save money, and by liberals who consider only the parents' discomfort. Neither conservatives nor liberals take pains to view abuse from the child's point of view.

4

THE UNDERCLASS

The modern child welfare and juvenile justice systems, established almost a century ago, have failed to live up to the expectations of their founders. The systems are a mess, floundering in a philosophy geared for the reality of the early twentieth century and fine-tuned by the mentality of the 1960s. In the next few chapters I suggest modest revisions which from my point of view—mired in the fray at the bottom of the valley—could bring about a modicum of reform.

But I do not pretend that doing away with archaic laws of confidentiality, turning much of what the courts now do over to social workers, encouraging interracial substitute care, or providing more residential placement opportunities will cure our troubled child welfare bureaucracies. The primary reason our child welfare system stinks has less to do with its philosophy, secrecy, or methods than with the nature of the families it attempts to help. Underclass children and families, cabined, cribbed, and confined by no-exit signs, differ substantially from poor children and families who hope—even expect—to escape from poverty.

I once represented Charles. No more. You can't represent a dead person. But cases like Charles's—and they're not rare —make me lean back and look out my window at Chicago's crumbling West Side and wonder what I'm accomplishing, other than taking home a paycheck every other week. For that matter, what good are the judges, prosecutors, public defenders, court reporters, bailiffs, and janitors doing here? Or the social workers and child welfare experts? Do we all end up fiddling with accidents and procedures because we don't, can't, grapple with the essence of what we are mired in?

What I do now isn't all that different from what I did thirty years ago as a young prosecutor, which drove me to Somalia. Young guys went and still go to jail for crimes they committed and will continue to commit after their release, and which they pretty much commit as will their offspring because they have no jobs and hence no money, and they have no jobs because they are dumb, and dumb because they have no education and dropped out of high school—actually dropped out mentally in grammar school, because no parent was around to kick them in the butt to go to school, and the parent didn't encourage education since she saw no need for it because her parent didn't see the need, and when the boy became almost a man no real man was around to deal with the almost-man's male aspirations, and his mom had other kids with no dads to deal with, so the boy became a man by himself (which normally is not a real good idea), and so no one was too surprised when he went to the joint for stealing other people's property or selling drugs for money or killing a friend he'd rather not have killed if he weren't drunk or stoned or pissed off and his friend wasn't drunk or stoned or pissed off and hadn't insulted him—though as he sits in his dank cell, he really can't recall what his friend said to piss him off.

And what do we do here for Charles, his brothers, sisters, mother, the father he never had, and the 55,000 or so other Charleses? We have a hell of a lot more judges (better ones, for that matter), more lawyers, social workers, psychiatrists, psychologists, and more money. But still the Charleses deluge our child welfare courts and agencies, and still we argue over how much due process or family preservation or family reunification or counseling or termination or adoption services we must provide. But each of us down deep knows we are ignoring, avoiding, or at most ineffectually touching the real issues and problems.

Like Charles. He was twelve, with a brother fourteen. They hung together. Like my own two boys, they were the best of friends one moment, the worst of enemies the next. But as against the rest of the world, even their mom, they became a unity. Like a lot of adolescent and preadolescent boys, they were hypersensitive to the taunts of other boys and girls. They were sensitive about the castoffs they wore, even more sensitive because the clothes were rancid, which brought other kids' taunts. The mother couldn't get her life together enough to go to the laundromat, or, as she told them, she just didn't have enough money. No crime to be poor, she'd say. But the boys knew better. Oh, they knew they were poor, even by neighborhood standards. Dirt poor. But they also knew that mom's longtime heroin addiction was a bottomless pit that sucked up every spare nickel and dime she could scrounge up.

More and more often the boys ditched school and roamed the streets. Mom wouldn't have gone along with the truancy, but she didn't know, her brain having become increasingly gelatinous. One day the brother became depressed. He said he was hungry; they had no food. Mom said she had no money to buy food. The boys were hungry all the time, but they were hungry for more than food. Charles looked on as his fourteen-year-old brother hung himself.

Shortly after his brother's death, Charles and his mother began living on the streets. The state intervened and took Charles away, placing him with his sister. A few months later the mother went into a nursing home. She was fifty years old.

Charles's sister was twenty-nine. She lived in the projects with five of her seven kids (the other two had died in infancy). The sister had been on welfare since her first child was born when she was fifteen. She had never worked for a paycheck. At one point the state child welfare agency claimed that the sister had been neglecting her children. It took the kids and placed them with her heroin-addicted mother, who herself had lost her children to a cousin for a while when the sister was young and before Charles was born.

The father of five of the sister's children was dead, having been killed by one of Charles's brothers. That brother is now on death row for killing his common-law brother-in-law and another man. Another brother is at the same prison doing twelve years for home invasion. Charles's other sister is also on welfare with her three kids, living in the same housing project, down the hall from the sister with whom Charles lived.

Shortly after Charles went to live with his sister, she caught a bullet in the stomach. She wasn't the intended victim, she was just in the wrong place at the wrong time during a gang shoot-out. She recovered, but a year later Charles, then fourteen, the same age as his brother when he hung himself, also happened to be in the wrong place at the wrong time. Well, not really. He was at school. But in some neighborhoods, school can be the wrong place at the wrong time. A kid shot off a couple of rounds, and one found Charles's head. He died instantly.

Charles's mother was then fifty-two, living on the public dole in a tiny corner of a bleak nursing home. In the not distant future she will no doubt mercifully die. Drugs ruined her brain, but a lot more went into crushing her spirit: two boys dying violently before they became men; two sons who became men, one to while away a major portion of his life in prison, the second to die there violently, just like the two men whose lives he snuffed out; two daughters, each of whom had children when they were not much older than Charles and his brother when they died, and each of whom has never been employed, probably never will be; and eight grandchildren living in the projects, ready to recycle the lives of their moms, dads, uncles, and grandma.

This is a worst-case scenario, but worst-case scenarios abound in the underclass. Worse-case situations are now legion and bad-case scenarios increasingly the rule. Those of us who work within the system engulfed by the Niagara of abused children call out in desperation and rage for more money and more programs. Sometimes the legislatures listen, and we get more judges, lawyers, social workers, bailiffs, court reporters, counselors, and janitors. But abused, neglected, and crack-addicted kids continue to flood the system, creating more jobs for middle-class child welfare types and advocates and a burgeoning industry of foundation-, university-, or government-supported pundits to advise us that we need more family preservation or community centers or night basketball or job training for grammar-school-dropout thirty-year-old grandmothers. Or other seers who tell us, just cut a mother's welfare after two or five years, or don't give her any money for additional children, and poof, she'll magically get a job—you know, the kind my grandparents got when they came from Europe but that are now in Indonesia.

In the sixties and seventies we thought the situation we read about in Michael Harrington's *The Other America* was desperate. Then, when I climbed the stairs of housing projects and visited tenements on Chicago's South and West sides, I knew firsthand the bleak lives of the poor. But these were the good old days when the poor were just poor and not underclass, and when we felt no fear in walking inner-city streets or negotiating housing project stairwells. Today, two and a half underclass generations later, I compare the underclass I see in court today with the poor I represented twenty-five or thirty years ago, and the comparison is invidious. No fathers. Never fathers. Schools that do not and cannot without parental involvement educate; empty factories in the inner city; a welfare system that deprives people of dignity, fostering irresponsible behavior and belittling self-discipline; drugs sold on street corners as freely as soda, and guns as available as the drugs; and the whole mess a Gordian knot resisting solutions and ready to explode in the outer city as random violence and in the inner city as rioting and looting.

A young Department of Labor economist named Daniel Moynihan publicized all this in the 1960s, but white and black liberals placed his report outside the ambit of public discourse by the simple device of branding it as racist— though they never argued that the raw facts he reported were untrue. Instead, as the messes of the underclass raged out of control, Democrats blamed Ronald Reagan and his revolution. It really wasn't a revolution at all, but it has given the Democrats a convenient excuse for all the social ills facing the country. Reagan was not exactly Oscar material, but it's only fair for liberals to blame him for the underclass mess. After all, conservatives have been excoriating Lyndon Johnson's expansive and "irresponsible" programs for the past thirty years for causing the plight of the poor. But it is a bit hypocritical for the liberals to shirk their responsibility since it was they who hushed up the Moynihan report when he tried to warn us of the coming maelstrom.

Moynihan argued that the growing trend of black children raised without fathers would ultimately lead to catastrophe. The left shouted him down because they feared racists would use Moynihan's report as proof that black people were less moral, ethical, and family-oriented than whites. Many on the right felt that way to begin with, so they didn't pay much attention to Moynihan or his report. Moynihan had the audacity to pick up a large rock, uncovering a thousand nasty, crawling creatures. We shoved the rock back in place, but the problems were still there. And they grew and multiplied.

Moynihan's report was straightforward and unspectacular. Using census tracks, he pointed out an accelerating trend of black children being born without the benefit of a male in the home. The figure had doubled in the previous decade or so, and by 1965, 25 percent of all black children were being born to single women. Today the rock can no longer cover the ugly fact that 68 percent of all black children are born to single women. In hard-core underclass neighborhoods that serve as a pipeline to the juvenile and criminal courts, the figure is over 95 percent.

Some, mostly academics, argue that a man in the home is not all that important, and that children who delay childbirth may not gain much. Reviewing a book by a sociology professor at Berkeley, a Yale sociologist argues that it is cruel to tell a poor girl to put off childbearing for a year or two, because she will gain little economically. The argument is that these kids are already so far down that delaying childbirth will not affect their lives and futures.

But if a fifteen-year-old girl delays having a child for two years, she might be able to finish two more years of school. In most cases she will certainly be a bit more mature. Hence the seventeen-year-old might decide to wait two more years so that she can further her education or go back to high school or get a General Education Degree. In many cases the two-year delay in childbearing will end up being more than two years. The girl-turned-young-woman may ultimately find a decent fellow who will stay around to be a father to her child.

The Yale sociologist goes on to suggest that the life of the mother (and presumably the child) "would not on the average improve very much even if the father agreed to join her in marriage. . . ." He argues that because the father most likely will be poor and without future prospects, any union could likely be a failure.

Perhaps so by Yale and Berkeley standards. The poor young couple will not have the resources for intensive conversations at upscale restaurants, nor the luxury to read, exercise, and watch art films. Instead the poor couple will probably both work eight- to ten-hour menial jobs, go back to their walk-up flat, eat fatty foods, and watch TV with a six-pack for entertainment. Life for poor families is tough. But it's a lot better, particularly for the children, than life in the underclass. There's a big difference between the poor and the underclass: poor kids can have futures.

In May 1994 the *New York Times* profiled twenty-six children age fifteen or under who had been charged with murder in New York City. More than twenty times, the phrase "the child had no involved father" leaped out of the text. Two profiles were silent as to the presence of a father. Only four children seemed to have any kind of father.

Still the left ducks the issue. On Mother's Day 1994 the director of the Children's Defense Fund, a good woman who certainly must know better, wrote, ". . . And if it's wrong for 13-year-old inner-city girls to have babies without benefit of marriage, it's wrong for rich celebrities too." Horsebleep. Thirteen-year-old inner-city (or suburban or rural) girls are eleven years removed from diapers and pacifiers themselves. They are not young women. They are children and will be so just once in their lives. They should be opening their minds to literature, mathematics, computers, sports, and dancing. Diapers; babies wailing in the middle of the night; Women, Infant and Children funds for baby formula; food stamps; and public aid lead to loneliness and frustration and the need for more adult and male companionship—and ultimately to more babies and more diapers. An older, more mature woman may decide to have and raise a child without a father. Given adequate resources, she will be a decent parent. A thirteen-year-old girl cannot be compared to "rich celebrities" or, for that matter, to any mature woman.

A few years ago I attended a meeting called by the news director of the local affiliate of one of the major television networks. In the wake of the highly publicized deaths of several children in Chicago, the director had pulled together people active in child welfare. He generously offered television time to educate the public about the problem of child abuse and its proposed remedies.

About thirty of us sat around a long heavy oak table in a luxurious boardroom. I was enjoying myself because the buffet table was loaded with good strong coffee, gourmet sweet rolls, and fresh fruit and juices. Then the meeting started. When the director asked for our suggestions, one of the first out of the starting blocks was an articulate, intense attorney for a well-known civil rights organization. She quickly set the boundaries. This is not a racial issue, she announced. As many white children as black are abused. The station would be acting irresponsibly if it showed only instances of black children being abused. Just about everyone in the room nodded in agreement.

When my turn came I pointed out that race was the overriding issue. Cook County, which includes Chicago, is about one-third black, yet 88 percent of the abuse and neglect cases at Juvenile Court involve African-American children while only 12 percent involve white or Hispanic children. The same situation bogs down child welfare and criminal justice systems in every major city in the United States. I pointed out that if we removed the so-called underclass from the equation, the attorney from the civil rights organization was correct. But the underclass—primarily black in our major cities because of our blighted history of slavery, segregation, and employment discrimination—*is* the equation. These statistics simply cannot be ignored, no matter what one's point of view. If a hard-core group of very poor folks, the underclass, cause a disproportionate amount of abuse and crime, we ought to take a hard look at this group and try to do something about their bleak existence. Or if the laws are stacked against this class of individuals so that they are unfairly sucked into the criminal and juvenile justice systems, we ought to examine this and, again, do something about it.

The social workers, child welfare types, and lawyers sitting around the table coughed, blew noses, scraped chairs, sipped coffee, stared at their hands, or scratched stick figures on yellow pads. The news director diplomatically moved on. Knowing I was defeated, I waited fifteen minutes or so and then left, explaining I had to be in court. But the coffee and rolls were great.

Harvard professor William Julius Wilson states the race issue more emphatically in his most recent book when he compares Hispanic and specifically Mexican households with African-American households. "Whereas 44 percent of the black women living with their children in Chicago's inner city have no other adults in the household, only 6.5 percent of comparable Mexican women are the sole adults in their households. Also, inner-city black women whose children are under twelve years of age are eight times more likely than comparable Mexican women to live in a single-adult household." Elsewhere Professor Wilson observes that as of 1993, 31 percent of all black children under age eighteen were living with a never-married parent while only 13 percent of Hispanic children and 5 percent of white children lived with a never-married parent. Wilson becomes more specific with Chicago: ". . . 47 percent of black parents in the inner city of Chicago have never been married, compared with 14 percent of the Mexican parents, 18 percent of the white parents, and 30 percent of the Puerto Rican parents."

Experiences in Cook County pretty much confirm Wilson's analysis. For instance, 88 percent of all children in the custody of the child welfare system in the county are black and only 6 percent are Hispanic, despite the fact that approximately 20 percent of Cook County's residents are Hispanic as against about a third who are black.

A few months after an eleven-year-old boy shot and killed a fourteen-year-old girl in Chicago, two boys, ten and eleven, tossed five-year-old Eric out the window of a fourteen-story housing project. Eric had refused to steal candy for them.

These kids were not born killers. While their environment certainly didn't help their maturation and contributed to their dysfunction, the vast majority of ten- and eleven-year-old kids in housing projects do not throw five-year-old boys to their deaths. These kids just happen to have lousy parents.

But after the two were sentenced to a juvenile penal facility, the liberal establishment bemoaned their fate. A well-known author who earlier had written about the downside of growing up in a housing project wrote about the conviction in the *New York Times* in a piece entitled, "It Takes a Village to Destroy a Child." According to this author, it was we, "the village guardians who failed them."

Self-described child advocates have sloganized "it takes a village to raise a child" in order to relieve bad parents of blame for abusing their children or of the responsibility for raising them as adequately as their resources permit. Indeed, "it takes a village" has become an incantation to ward off those who dare suggest that with parenthood comes individual responsibility, even for overwhelmed adolescent parents who should not have had the children in the first place. Taken in context, as Hillary Rodham Clinton did in her book of the same name, the "village" proverb has meaning. As a society we cannot turn our backs on children whose parents are inadequate, or the poor or mentally disabled, or those who, for reasons beyond their control, are unable to reach their potential. And these folks include some abusive parents who are willing to accept responsibility for their actions and ultimately to accept the responsibilities of parenthood.

The "village" can—should—provide support for families, but the village is not responsible for nurturing the children. That's the job of a committed parent, hopefully two committed parents. The most insensitive right-wing racist does not cause half the damage for the inner-city poor as do their self-proclaimed advocates. The argument that "they're just poor victims," as a defense of the crimes and foibles of a minority of the underclass and a tinier percentage of the poor, leaves the public to infer that all poor people are criminals, welfare junkies, and child abusers. The advocates of course do not intend this damage, but they half-believe that the poor are irresponsible victims who need their protection. That's because these advocates have contact only with poor criminals, thieves, mental patients, and parents who abuse their children. Like Plato's man chained to the cave wall, they view the poor only by way of incomplete images.

The village must protect children whose parents have failed them either purposefully, because of neglect, or for reasons beyond their control. And the village should help poor families with programs, funds, and jobs. The village can indeed provide a family with a friendly environment, but only a parent can raise a child.

Welfare reform is a highly complex and controversial subject, but it has become increasingly clear that there is a connection between the underclass and a welfare system that encourages irresponsible behavior. In June 1994, as Republicans pushed a draconian welfare reform package and President Clinton suggested a more modest approach, this item appeared in the *Chicago Tribune*:

"There is a danger that [Clinton's plan] will treat children very poorly," said . . . , professor in the University of Chicago School of Social Work.

Recalling the squalid scene last February when 19 children were found living in a garbage-ridden Keystone apartment on Chicago's west side, . . . said, "Here in Chicago, I think we already have a taste of what's likely to be the impact."

We represented the nineteen—actually twenty-six—Keystone children. Welfare reform had nothing to do with their problems or the case. In February 1994 Chicago police broke into a suspected crack house on Chicago's West Side, expecting to be greeted by gun-toting drug addicts. Instead they interrupted two toddlers in dirty diapers on a cold floor, grappling with a dog over a bone. The cops holstered their weapons and plowed through the rest of the filthy two-bedroom apartment, uncovering blankets, garbage, dirty clothes, human feces, rat droppings, and seventeen other children either sleeping on the floor or crammed atop two soiled mattresses. The walls had gaping holes, the toilet was broken, the kitchen stove didn't work. Rotting food crusted the shelves of the refrigerator, and there was nothing in the place anyone could eat.

Six sisters, the oldest thirty-one and the youngest twenty, lived in the apartment with nineteen of their twenty-six children. The other seven lived with various relatives. None of the nineteen fathers played a significant role in their children's lives. The police filed criminal and abuse charges against the mothers. Then came headlines and TV footage, followed quickly by apologists who defended the women as victims of poverty. But their arguments did not explain the cuts, bruises, belt marks, and cigarette burns on a four-year-old boy's body. Nor could the women's defenders explain what happened to more than $6,000 a month in various welfare benefits that poured into the apartment. Based upon the sisters' criminal records, it is not irrational to believe that most of the money was going up someone's nose or into someone's arm.

Welfare reform, being only a gleam in the eye of possible progenitors, had no impact on the Keystone case or hundreds of similar cases we see each week. Keystone made the headlines because the sisters and the kids lived together. Ordinarily they would be living separately but with identical scenarios: teenage pregnancies, high school or grammar school dropout moms, no dads, no jobs, and too much drugs, booze, or both. A legitimate question hovers over such cases: Will reforming the welfare system ameliorate these cases or make them worse?

The left argues that job training, child care, and jobs will resolve much underclass misery. Two social workers wrote in September 1993: "If there were good job training, adequate child care and decent wages at the end of the road, many women would eagerly leave welfare. Such programs would cost upward of fifty billion, so that it is not what government is doing. Instead, the harassment of welfare mothers in the name of reform continues."

This kind of sloppy thinking helped get us into our present predicament. The welfare mother is not hostage to her irresponsible behavior. She is demonized by the village which, being the *real* responsible parent, must bail her out with baby-sitting, job training, and a guarantee of decent employment. I would support this kind of thinking if there were any proof it works. But we've had job training programs in the past, and while they have succeeded with some, to a large degree they have failed. And for good reason. The place for job training is in grammar school, high school, even college.

School-oriented reformers have for years argued that more money for more and better schools will improve underclass conditions. Children of the underclass will claw their way out of their culture in traditional fashion, like earlier immigrant groups, through education. In recent years government has poured billions of dollars into new and better schools, hardware, and teachers. And dropout rates have increased and the underclass population multiplied.

Now school reformers argue for still more money for education, ignoring countless studies demonstrating that inner-city private and parochial schools with pinched resources turn out better students with exceedingly low dropout rates. Reformers often dismiss these studies, arguing that parochial and private schools can pick and choose their students while the public schools must take all comers.

Inner-city parochial and private schools usually have strict discipline codes which force students to sit down, open books, and learn. More important, their students' parents are concerned and motivate their kids—or kick butt. They are not shelling out thousands of dollars for F's and absenteeism. If only one-third of public school parents don't give a damn, that allows their kids to pollute the atmosphere for the other two-thirds. Under these circumstances, is it surprising that many of these remaining two-thirds will be swayed by peer pressure to give up school?

A recent comprehensive study confirmed what most of us know instinctively, that the most critical influence on students' performance in school is their parents and peers. As reported in the *New York Times* in August 1996, a ten-year study surveyed twenty thousand students in the ninth through twelfth grades, and their families, for one to three years. One of the authors of the report, Dr. Laurence Steinberg, a psychology professor at Temple University and an expert on families with teenagers, commented, "We think the school reform movement has been focusing on the wrong things. The problem isn't the schools; it's the disengagement of parents and a peer culture that demeans high academic performance." This is an ominous message because the underclass needs job skills in order to pull itself out of the morass. The vast majority do acquire these skills in their formative years, particularly in grammar school and high school. But teen parents without helpful companions frequently have additional children and quickly become overwhelmed. They do not motivate their children, whose lives ultimately mirror those of their parents.

We can never pour enough money into schools. But underfunded schools will turn out good students (as inner-city private and parochial schools do) as long as parents are interested in their children's education and willing to motivate them to learn. As Dr. Steinberg pointed out, "No curriculum overhaul, no instructional innovation, no change in school organization, no toughening of standards, no rethinking of teacher training or compensation will succeed if students do not come to school interested in and committed to learning."

Only so many resources are available. Rather than scatter them among a variety of programs benefiting, in the long run, middle-class bureaucrats, we should emphasize programs that encourage children to stay in school and discourage stupid decisions that will hound them for the rest of their lives. Instead of making the poor irresponsible victims, society should demand the same excellence of underclass children that we expect from suburban children. Now, unless a kid is six feet two inches, weighs 220 pounds, and runs like the wind, we demand nothing of him.

Family involvement must remain the cornerstone of the education, particularly the early education, of most children. But many parents do not understand the connection between adequate education and job opportunity—and for good reason. Poor blacks still suffer discrimination, even more than underclass blacks.

Too many underclass parents do not motivate their children because they are lost in a fourth-world culture in which it is common to drop out of the educational experience either in the later years of grammar school or the early years of high school. Their children, not being motivated, do not learn well unless they are geniuses, increasingly do poorly at school, and cause annoyances that prevent many other children, whose parents do motivate them, from learning. Meanwhile our inner-city school systems, like giant vacuums, suck up more and more money while turning out less and less.

While it is easy to blame the school system rather than the parents, school systems do share some of the responsibility for this situation. They woodenly respond to the complexities of educating children of the underclass. The earlier and more sustained are educational opportunities for children, particularly children of the underclass, the better they will do. Early and sustained education is essential.

And our big-city school systems should be flexible enough to permit adolescents to move from an academic to a nonacademic setting in order to receive training in a variety of job opportunities. Many kids are turned off to Shakespeare, algebra, and world history. They *should* learn these things, and perhaps will later. But rather than have them walk out the school door and become pregnant or involved with gangs, the schools must respond to the expectations and potential of bored, apathetic adolescents. Schools could be connected to businesses where adolescents might work part-time while being trained. The kid could even earn a modest sum below the minimum wage in exchange for his or her services.

Recently a University of Chicago social work professor argued that the crisis with welfare dependency and teenage births need not alarm us. Echoing other advocates, she pointed out that only 7 percent of the welfare caseloads consists of people on AFDC for more than six years, and that families headed by a woman under age eighteen constitute less than 1.5 percent of Illinois's AFDC caseload. The nation, she declared, spends only $16 billion a year on welfare.

These figures and others like them are misleading because they consider *all* people who receive welfare. The Bane/Ellwood studies from Harvard University debunk this approach. Most people get on the welfare rolls because of a crisis and quickly get out. Bane and Ellwood point out that to truly understand our welfare system we must study who is on welfare at any one point in time rather than consider all people who ever pick up a single welfare check. When the statistics are reviewed from one point in time, the results confirm the plight of the underclass. At any one time more than *half* of all people on welfare have been on welfare more than eight years. Further, 29.4 percent of all individuals on welfare are under age twenty-two while 37 percent are between twenty-two and thirty. Read together, these statistics demonstrate that a substantial number of young women have babies as teenagers and remain on welfare as they mature into their twenties.

The cost of welfare is much more than the $16 billion spent annually on Aid to Families with Dependent Children. When medical subsidies, food stamps, and other benefits are considered, the actual cost is well over $150 billion a year. Even at this figure the cost of welfare is not astronomical in terms of the nation's budget. But the cost of welfare is devastating in related consequences, such as children ending up in the criminal justice system, abused and neglected or simply living out their lives in despair and ultimately on welfare themselves. To understand the dependent culture that welfare has spawned, the underclass, and the problems of this class, legislators and academicians need not read or cite statistics. Instead they should spend a few days or weeks in our big-city criminal and juvenile courts.

I have been involved in the criminal and juvenile justice systems for more than three decades. In 1968 there were fewer than 2,000 abused and neglected children in our Juvenile Court. Between 1983 and 1986 the number increased but stabilized at about 8,000. By 1991 it had increased to 20,000. Today more than 40,000 abused and neglected children are in the custody of the child welfare system in Cook County. Over 90 percent of these children are born to women on welfare, and at least 80 percent have no involved father. Nationally the figures are equally depressing. Between 1983 and 1996 the numbers of children in child welfare systems has just about doubled, from approximately 250,000 to half a million. The states of California, New York, and Illinois harbor almost 40 percent of all children in substitute care nationally, or about 180,000 children.

Many argue that children do not have children in order to get welfare money. True in most cases. But the problem is not economic, it is cultural. Over the past thirty years a fourth-world culture has evolved in the United States that is much worse than anything I saw when I lived in a so-called third-world country in Africa. This underclass culture is comprised of poor people but is not the culture of the poor. Some do not like the term "underclass," but it is as good a word as any to describe people who are poor and live with other poor people, but who for reasons largely beyond their control are different and often prey on poor people. The major difference between most poor people in this country and most middle-class people is one of money. The difference between the underclass and the rest of the country, including other poor people, is one of culture as well as money. Underclass children have children simply because it is part of their culture.

By spotlighting welfare reform we have avoided the real issue—a dysfunctional fourth-world culture that strangles its young. We dare not discuss this culture openly because its members are disproportionately black. Like Moynihan's mid-sixties report, we push the nasty underclass problems under a rock. But is it racist to discuss the issues honestly, or is it racist to yell *racist* at anyone who wants to pick up the rock and bring the problems into the open?

Ignoring the problems of the underclass, or pretending that a few additional welfare dollars or a training class for a thirty-year-old ninth-grade dropout grandma will abruptly turn her life around is fatuous. The underclass is possessed by demons of teenage children, absent fathers, substandard schooling, lack of employment, drugs, and violence which will not easily be exorcised. Those who suppress this debate are not intentionally racist. For the most part they are the major apologists and advocates for the black underclass. But in my judgment they are short-sighted and harm the very people they would help.

In September 1994 Oprah Winfrey announced she would finance a program to move one hundred families out of public housing, off public aid, and into better lives. The program, Families for a Better Life, was to be administered through one of Chicago's premier social service agencies, the Jane Addams Hull House Association. Ms. Winfrey promised $3 million and the freedom to spend it without government red tape.

But according to the *Chicago Tribune*, after two years and $1.3 million only five families had completed the program. The project was put on hold. The *Tribune* reported, "At its most basic the lesson of Families for a Better Life may be that the lives of the poor are so chaotic and infused with a 'mind

frame of entitlement' that they defy even programs specifically designed to overcome these obstacles."

After Ms. Winfrey announced the program, more than
thirty thousand people applied. Only about sixteen hundred
returned completed applications out of four thousand who
met the requirements that they live in public housing in
Chicago. The staff then culled out anyone with drug involvement or a criminal background. According to the vice-
president for planning at Hull House, "welfare mentality"
remained an obstacle. "Even though we carefully screened
them, there was the mind frame of entitlement. We had to
keep emphasizing that this is not about what you get. This is
about what you do."

One of the findings was that "adults who didn't have high
school education or any significant job experience had so
much trouble finding and keeping work that the program
could not set them firmly on their feet within a time frame designed to quickly foster self-sufficiency." Hull House officials
decided that in the future they would require all participants
to have either a high school diploma or their G.E.D. Of course,
by definition most people in the underclass have neither.

In 1996 President Clinton signed a welfare reform measure that was pretty much a Republican package. In doing so
he stated that while the measure was not perfect, it was a necessary beginning that could be adjusted in the coming years.
His critics, mostly fellow Democrats, argued that he had
caved in to political pressures and had signed the bill only
because 1996 was an election year. Whatever his motives, I
think the president did the right thing. And he is correct that
as we determine the failings of the bill, we can tinker with it.

The bill abolishes the federal guarantee of welfare benefits and instead gives the states block grants to use as they wish. The bill's critics claim that the states do not have the steel to do the job and that as many as a million children will go homeless or hungry. But children are already suffering, and if welfare were to continue as before, more and more children would suffer. There would be more teenage mothers, more grandmothers in their late twenties or early thirties, more cases of children raised without any idea of what a father is, more crime, more dependency, and a future full of more of the same. Something drastic must be done to turn the fourth-world underclass culture around. The Welfare Reform Bill may not be perfect, but it is a beginning.

The bill also provides that if the youngest child is over the age of five, the mother should be required to work within two years of receiving benefits. The mother and the children are guaranteed health coverage under Medicaid as long as they qualify for welfare. A single mother whose youngest child is under age five is exempt from work requirements if she demonstrates that she cannot find suitable and affordable child care. A single mother under age eighteen must live with an adult and attend school in order to receive welfare benefits, unless she or her child is likely to suffer serious physical or emotional harm as a result of the living arrangement. Finally, a woman is required to provide information about the father of her child as a condition to receiving welfare. If she does not cooperate with the state authorities, she will lose at least one-quarter of her family's welfare benefit. The new law sets a five-year lifetime limit for aid from the federal block grants.

The main purpose of welfare reform must be to slice into the culture of dependency and leave the message that there is a place for job training. It is called school. Education is the starting point for a better life. Government will not be around forever to offer the illusion of (marginal) help.

The preclusion of additional benefits does not prevent women from having additional children, but it does force the same economic realities upon the underclass that the rest of us have. No one criticizes a working mother and father who look at their budget and decide to use various forms of birth control in order to delay or avoid having children. Arguing that the village must give more money to irresponsible parents who have more children simply labels the underclass as victims and tells them that society will reward them for irresponsible behavior.

I cannot pretend to know what will eradicate the underclass culture. I can state the obvious: girls having babies before they are women, with men or boys who seldom accept the responsibility of fatherhood, places an enormous and unfair burden on the children. Society's efforts at ameliorating the lives of these children and their parents frequently create and perpetuate dependency. The bureaucracies we have built to work with the poor and the allies of these bureaucracies in academia and government unions blindly push for more resources. These ultimately benefit the middle-class providers of services but most often have little or even a negative impact on the people for whom the services are intended.

Plans and programs meant to assist the underclass should be aimed at creating self-sufficiency and a climate of achievement. Social service agencies today clamor for more community service centers at which the poor would be assisted by social workers. But as useful as such community service centers are, much more useful are jobs in the inner city. For instance, the Chicago Housing Authority recently developed a program in response to welfare reform, contracting some of its services to tenant-owned businesses. According to the *New York Times*, under the rules of the program, tenants must own at least 51 percent of the company in order to be eligible for the small business program and housing authority loans and contracts. One company, already formed in response to the program, has a $730,000 contract to clean seventeen Housing Authority buildings. Of the forty-eight people employed, 80 percent are public housing residents. The salaries range from $5.50 to $9 per hour; the jobs include mopping floors, sweeping stairwells, polishing elevators, changing lightbulbs, and scrubbing toilets.

Although for every three dollars they earn on their jobs they lose one dollar in public assistance, the workers are entitled to keep government health and child-care benefits. And, unlike some make-work programs, this one is tough on its workers. According to the woman who runs it, herself a public housing resident, about ten people have been fired in the past year for abusing drugs and alcohol and for absences and lateness. "Our backs aren't strong enough to carry a bunch of folks, so we don't try," she told the *New York Times*.

A twenty-six-year-old mother of three told the reporter, "I never had anything to fall back on. Now, I can see a future for me and my kids." One doubts if she would be saying this after a visit to a community service center.

In Juvenile Court, parents who have abused their children

are frequently sent to parenting classes. I have always thought this was a waste. The time to teach people when to parent is when they themselves are children. Classes ought to be held regularly for all children at the grammar school and high school levels, concentrating on the responsibilities of parenthood. Children are now exposed to various drug- and alcohol-abuse classes which seem to be bearing fruit. Children should be instructed about the importance of fathers and the need to forge a constructive life before having children. If parents do not wish to have their children attend these classes, they can, as in the case of sex education courses, sign a waiver.

Family planning, in concept and techniques, should be as available in the inner city as it is now to the rest of us. Ironically the same self-proclaimed saints who lament the underclass and its problems often enforce a rigid philosophy upon the poor which excludes access to birth-control techniques.

Eliminating the underclass culture will be an exceedingly difficult task, particularly since it is so locked up with issues of race in our major cities. But for the sake of those people who are forced to live lives of misery surrounded by crime and joblessness, we must do it. And we must have the candor to address the real issues. In the long run, intelligent investment will pay off in lower expenditures for prison cells, foster homes, and the child welfare system in general.

5

THE CONFIDENTIALITY GAME

I sometimes watch one of those *sincere* talk shows the local public television station airs between the bird and bunny specials. You know, the ones that show close-ups of flies having sex, or birds wolfing down worms, or a family of gorillas romping through a jungle clearing. In fact, the copulating flies are often more interesting than the talk shows, where a pompous, intense host lets his guest and the general public in on his intelligence and humanity as he asks long-winded questions.

One evening I channel-surfed my way to the talk show, where the guests included several child advocates. How do we fix the child welfare system and what's the price tag? was the essence of one question. The responses included establishing community-centered settlement houses where social workers, parenting classes, child care, after-school programs, drug rehab, and night basketball would do away with child abuse and underclass depression. Another suggested a model used in New Zealand, where elders and cousins have rap sessions with child abusers. A third insisted that child abuse was a figment of middle-class America's imagination, that most people accused of abusing their children were simply poor folks needing services. The price tag, all agreed, was irrelevant.

All these responses view inner-city misery from a middle-class perspective. The first and third of them lump all inner-city poor together. Community-centered settlement houses are great for the inner city. But most folks who take advantage of these centers are the vast majority of decent people who do not abuse their kids. A twenty-two-year-old with four kids, no high school education, no involved father for her kids, and suffering from a reality-based depression may be able to get to the local crack dealer (who's probably just outside her door) but may not have the wherewithal to get her kids to the community center. But if she had made it to the community center when she was nine years old, maybe someone there could have influenced her life before it got turned around the wrong way. In the long run, community-based settlement programs are an expensive but important way to bring about minimal reform.

I have no problem with the New Zealand plan except that there are more sheep than people in New Zealand. There's probably more misery on one floor of one housing project on Chicago's South Side or in New York's South Bronx or South Central Los Angeles than in the islands of New Zealand.

Had the sincere long-winded fellow asked me, I could have given him some suggestions for reform. And the price tag would be popular: no cost. Well, no money but perhaps a red face here and there. Child welfare will never be reformed until the curtain of confidentiality shrouding the industry from public scrutiny is torn down.

Confidentiality was a cornerstone of the first juvenile courts founded about a century ago. And for good reason. The courts were to reform children whose adolescent pranks led to crime. Assuming the kid was reformed, the adolescent misadventure should not brand him a criminal for the rest of his life. When the juvenile courts assumed jurisdiction of abuse and neglect cases, the same laws of confidentiality crept into that arena as well. Nor was this illogical. Dysfunctional families that overcome their problems should be able to get on with their lives.

But by the time the 1890s became the 1990s, kids stealing apples or tossing rocks at the cop on the beat had evolved into children selling crack on corners for men and women, and sixteen-year-olds gunning down nine-year-olds in drive-by shootings with bullets meant for someone else.

The world has changed but the laws of confidentiality remain and, if anything, are tougher. In many states reporters are not permitted into juvenile courtrooms. In most states the general public has no access to the courtrooms, and in practically all states neither reporters nor the general public have access to juvenile court or child welfare files, even in cases where a child has been harmed as a result of government negligence.

What about the sanctity of children and their families? the child welfare crowd and their protectors, foundations, government unions, and the legislatures will argue. And what's happening to the kids and their families now? Well, what happened to Elisa Izquerdo?

In November 1995 six-year-old Elisa was tortured to death by her mother, to whom New York City child welfare officials had returned her despite warnings about mom's romance with crack. School social workers had informed child welfare workers that Elisa came back disoriented and bruised from overnight visits with her mother. After her death the *New York Times* reported that a "child welfare administration spokesperson said that state confidentiality laws prevented her from commenting on whether the agency had received these reports or acted upon them."

A year and a half earlier the *Times* had editorialized about four-year-old Shyana Bryant, also tortured and killed by her parents after she too had been returned to them not once but twice. Both Shyana and her sister had been born with cocaine in their systems and had been repeatedly abused. After Shyana's death, the child welfare administration assured the *Times* they were "conducting an internal investigation. But even if it wanted to publish the results, the state's confidentiality law prohibits disclosure . . . and inhibits accountability."

As I write this in 1996, Congress has several committees examining the president's role in Whitewater and his wife's role in the firing of White House travel consultants. Just a few weeks ago a congressional committee concluded weeks of questioning witnesses about the death of the wife of a paranoid right-wing militia nut during a standoff with law enforcement officers. For purposes of the media and hence the public, Congress rightfully spotlights every misstep, error, or statement of all possible witnesses in these cases. But the facts prompting social workers to return a six-year-old or a four-year-old to abusive parents and leave the kids there despite repeated warnings from professionals and others must be kept from the media and the public. The child and the family must be protected, and we the public are not sophisticated enough to comprehend. But not to worry. An internal secret audit will clear up the mess—for those intelligent enough to understand. Insiders.

When my office asked to see the Illinois child welfare agency's internal review of the death of a three-year-old child killed in foster care, the agency refused. Its public relations spokesperson explained: "DCFS must be able to look within itself to ascertain where there were failures to adequately protect our children and then determine the best method of correction. Prohibiting public access to private information might deprive newspapers of a few headlines and politicians of their opportunity to grandstand, but it has never interfered with legal proceedings in any way."

The agency's lawyer was even clearer in her obfuscation: "We are trying to maximize our ability to review a bad situation and to learn from any mistakes which may have occurred anywhere by anyone. . . . It is our view that there will be a chilling effect upon an open, frank discussion of the facts if the matter is not maintained in a confidential manner."

The child welfare crowd jabber the usual defenses in these cases, and some of them are legitimate. People will hesitate to inform on abusive parents, fearing disclosure. Good point. So protect the reporter of child abuse by placing her name in a separate sealed file.

An abused child's name should not be published. Okay. So mandate that the media may not use the child's name—which they seldom do anyway, unless, like Elisa, the kid has been kicked to death by her parent.

But at a minimum, if the state has received reports concerning child abuse, or if the state has moved to investigate that abuse and the child is later physically harmed or killed, the media should have complete access to every file (with the exception of the person who reported the abuse) available on that child, to use in whatever way they deem appropriate.

The media should have complete access to every juvenile courtroom and be able to report on what occurs there while normally withholding the names of children. The media, and members of the public for good cause, should also have access to files of children seriously harmed while in the substitute-care system.

Open government usually works. Even if it doesn't work on every occasion, it has the opportunity to work because the public, through the media, can scrutinize it and demand reform. Closed government, as we have seen in Eastern Europe and the former Soviet Union, usually fails.

The child welfare bureaucracies have tougher laws of confidentiality protecting their incompetence than any other government agency with the exception of the CIA. The reasons for this secrecy really have nothing to do with children or informants. The child welfare crowd needs to carry on its agenda protected from public scrutiny. And not scrutiny from its errors. Most child welfare workers and advocates are decent, dedicated, and highly motivated people. They would be glad to rid the profession of incompetents, though it is increasingly difficult because of government unions—that's another story. But child welfare insiders need their work shrouded from public awareness because they believe the public is incapable of understanding what they frequently do. And they are right.

Elisa Izquerdo and Shyana Bryant's stories must be kept from the public not because they reveal negligence within the child welfare bureaucracies but because they demonstrate just how the bureaucracies work and should work. These cases were not failures but successes. The patients just died.

Illinois's child welfare agency lobbied the legislature to set aside $20 million for a specific family preservation program called Family First. The legislature did this but also asked the University of Chicago's Chapin Hall to do a three-year study on Family First to determine its efficacy. In its report, Chapin Hall pointed out that DCFS officials recognized that the family preservation initiative would lead to the deaths of some children. But DCFS apparently believed that the successes would outweigh these setbacks. The report stated, "It is almost certain that the probability of child deaths will be higher in a program in which children at risk are left at home rather than taken into foster care. . . ." The report goes on to observe, "The original designers of the [family preservation program] realized that such cases would occur and went to some lengths to devise responses to these crises."

As part of the evaluation process, Chapin Hall gathered data on the deaths of children during and after Family First services. But after about a year Chapin Hall reported that "DCFS administrators have asked us to suspend our study of child deaths." In other words, since this was a legislative project, the report would be public. DCFS officials did not want an unsophisticated public to have information about kids who died while their parents received government largesse.

Later, after my office used the Chapin Hall report to get the legislature to reduce funds for Family First, DCFS admitted that six children had died while being served by this specific program. Incidentally, the report concluded that Family First kept *no* children out of the system and that the agency was spending $20 million to save $2 million—or, in effect, losing $18 million as well as six children. Nonetheless, in the best tradition of bureaucracy, the agency sought to expand the program.

What organization stands for open government and the public's right to know? The American Civil Liberties Union, of course. The ACLU is synonymous with the First Amendment. Well, not always. In the fall of 1993 one of its lawyers wrote a federal judge:

> It is difficult in a brief letter like this to describe all of the measures which are needed to deal with the broader issues causing the problems at [DCFS]. It is even more difficult to discuss these kinds of complex issues in open court status hearings every few months in which the par-

ties and the monitor speak briefly about one or two subjects in front of a room full of reporters. We therefore urge you to consider holding regular, in-chambers status hearings in addition to those in open court.

What material did the self-proclaimed defenders of the First Amendment wish to secrete in chambers, away from a room full of reporters and hence the public? The short story is that it had to do with the child welfare system and the ACLU's role in it. And the longer story?

Five years earlier the ACLU had sued DCFS on behalf of children in the system, in a class action which my office initially supported. But once we figured out what was happening, we vigorously opposed the suit. After several years of litigation, the lawsuit became a "friendly" lawsuit. The ACLU and the child welfare big shots discovered they essentially shared the same philosophy. The system needed more money to hire more caseworkers who would then be in a position to provide more services for more families and send more kids home where they belonged all along, because only the parents' poverty caused the mess in the first place. The major villain was the legislature, which hadn't funded the state's welfare agencies appropriately. So about a dozen folks, child welfare bureaucrats and ACLU lawyers, sat down together. They fashioned a federal consent judgment which forced the legislature to ante up.

To cover their deal, the ACLU and DCFS hired experts to "advise" them. Most of the experts were academics who shared the views of the ACLU and their child welfare counterparts. But in a couple of instances the experts went their own way. For example, in a paper on residential care, two hands-on people, Mary Ann Brown who runs Hephzibah, an outstanding orphanage for younger children in Oak Park, Illinois, and Dr. Earle P. Kelly, who ran a residential care facility in Iowa, argued that as part of a continuum of services, Illinois needed more residential beds both for younger children and adolescents. This view contradicted the conventional wisdom that children should be kept out of residential care, so their advice was ignored. As the federal judge on the case spelled out in a letter to a state senator who sought additional residential beds:

> As you know, the decree does not provide for orphanages or large group homes. Rather, it is directed toward reuniting children with their families, or if that proves inappropriate, adoption or foster placements in family type settings. It would be inappropriate for me to endorse any plan or procedure that would be contrary to the terms of the decree.

The chief counsel for the ACLU put it more succinctly when he told the *Chicago Sun-Times*, "Rather than take a child from a family because the house is ice cold, for example, the state could pay the heating bill. And rather than take a child from a parent who left the child unattended while running errands, the state could pay for a babysitter."

I do not disagree with the ACLU lawyer, who happens to be a decent and dedicated human being. But he has had little contact with the realities of the juvenile justice system. In the 1990s children are not removed from homes because their parents are too poor to pay the heating bills. At least I haven't seen a case like that in twenty years. Today homes are ice-cold because the parents spend every nickel they can find on drugs and leave the kids freezing and hungry. And mothers go out to shop and leave the kids at home alone. Again, these cases do not come to court. But many parents walk out on their kids for hours, days, and weeks, partying until either a fire starts or the grandma or uncle or aunt breaks in to save the kids.

The court judgment forced the agency to hire hundreds of additional workers on the theory that a larger bureaucracy would provide better services to parents, thus children could either remain at home or return more quickly. But no evidence supports the idea that a larger bureaucracy prevents parents from abusing their children, or better reforms them once they do. We too believed that the child welfare system needed more resources, but we felt they should have been directed toward more group homes, residential beds, and greater financial aid for those willing to adopt problem children. The federal judge's views to the contrary, frequently there is no home to which a child may be returned, no home to which a decent person would want to send a child.

The court ruled in December 1991. A respected former state judge was appointed to monitor the decree and report back to the court concerning its successes or failures. By 1995 the legislature had more than doubled the DCFS budget, from about $500 million to $1.2 billion. But the number of children pouring into the system had also doubled. Instead of returning children to their homes, the hiring of additional workers had brought more children into the system because more workers were investigating more hot-line calls. And every six months the monitor reported that the child welfare agency was "massively out of compliance" with the deadlines set in the court decree.

So on one hand things were going as intended. The legislature had poured hundreds of millions of dollars into the child welfare system, and the agency was trying to keep kids at home. On the other hand, things weren't working out at all. Kids were pouring into the system, and Juvenile Court judges had become much more sensitive to the downside of family preservation—in part, I like to think, because of the ruckus we had raised. The judges were more hesitant to send the children back to abusive parents; so the number of kids within the agency kept piling up. The ACLU argued that given more time the decree would work. But the media continued to report on DCFS's many failures and on the monitor's critical reports. So ACLU lawyers suggested that discussions concerning the court decree be held in chambers, outside the presence of "a room full of reporters."

After a number of private sessions in chambers, the judge decided that he no longer needed a monitor. He dismissed the former judge and dropped the requirement for six-month reports. So in 1996 the DCFS spent $1.2 billion under forced funding, for a plan drawn up by a few geniuses that affects some sixty thousand abused kids and every taxpayer in the state—without a neutral party to scrutinize the results. All decisions and reports are now ferreted away in the safety of the judge's chambers, away from "a room full of reporters."

Our office is appointed to act as a child's lawyer and guardian *ad litem*, which means that we also make decisions with respect to the course of litigation. I have interpreted this to mean that we have a right, indeed a responsibility, to speak out for these children who cannot speak out for themselves. This approach has not endeared us to Illinois's child welfare establishment. Once, while trying to get the legislature to make modest changes in the family preservation law, we were attacked by child advocates for "demonizing" poor women who required family preservation services. They claimed that we exaggerated the problems, that in fact the Illinois family preservation program was a success.

So I sent each legislator a picture of Siaonia's body on the medical examiner's slab with her vagina and anus burned off. The howls from the welfare establishment were deafening. They wrote the newspapers, went on television, and bombarded the editorial boards about my conduct. Not only was I a boor, but I had broken the law and violated the child's privacy rights by sending out pictures of her naked and tortured body.

The brutalized child's body of course had no privacy rights. But not one child advocate mentioned Siaonia's mother who murdered her, or her father who abandoned her, or her mother's boyfriend who took welfare money meant for her and stood by while mom beat and ultimately murdered her. No, I was the bad guy. I had let the world in on a dirty little secret that was really a success story gone sour.

A few years ago, eighteen-year-old Frank and I attended a settlement conference with a federal judge and DCFS's chief counsel. Frank had been with DCFS since he was two. I had sued the agency in federal court for violating his civil rights. A private agency that had cared for Frank for several years under a DCFS contract had recently settled. Recognizing their responsibility for some of his problems, they paid several hundred thousand dollars into a trust for the young man. Federal Judge Ilana Rovner ordered a settlement conference to determine if DCFS would also settle. Now, the state has a responsibility to the taxpayers not to settle a bad case. But the DCFS lawyer didn't argue that our case was unfounded. Instead he attacked Frank.

Not a dollar. Not a nickel. Not a penny. I can paraphrase his remarks but not the venom in his voice as he snarled that Frank was a *junkie, whore, thief.* The lawyer agreed to place Frank in a mental institution where he belonged, but he informed Judge Rovner that DCFS was considering suing Frank for the money the private agency had agreed to put away for him—because DCFS had spent a lot of taxpayer money on services for Frank over the previous sixteen years.

That evening, my two-year-old son Joey cried out. As I rocked him, I thought of those services. DCFS's files reported that between the ages of two and four, Frank and his sister lived with foster parents who locked them in a basement and tossed in baby food for them to eat. When Frank was four, DCFS figured something was wrong and removed the children. The kids went through several other foster homes in the next year or so. His mother dropped out of the picture. His father, a Vietnam veteran, had committed suicide. Frank had only his sister. When Frank was six, DCFS took her away from him.

A DCFS worker chronicled: "Frank was abruptly and, I think, inappropriately separated from his sister because of sexual play. . . . Quite a big deal was made of this, both at the time of the separation and again [later]." The foster mother had informed DCFS that the six- and five-year-olds had touched each other while bathing.

Frank continued moving through foster homes. When he was eight he told his social worker that his foster father played with his penis. She did not believe him. By the time he was thirteen he had been in and out of fifteen placements. A psychologist wrote, "Frank is a youngster whose multiple placement and rejection experiences have left him with a severe emotional handicap. He is presently unable to develop close personal relationships with others, especially parental figures. . . . The cycle of multiple placements *must be* stopped before this young man can work on overcoming his fear of social relationships . . ." (emphasis in the original). Instead he went through half a dozen other placements. In one he was sexually molested by a counselor. Then he was sent to mental institutions, welfare hotels, child-care centers, temporary shelter, and finally the streets.

The DCFS lawyer was right. Frank had committed crimes and had turned to drugs. He survived on the streets the only way the agency had taught him he had any worth: he turned tricks for men. (DCFS probably single-handedly keeps the prostitution trade going in Chicago with new male and female recruits. About half the older kids I represented at one time or another turned to hooking in order to live.) Frank stole. And he took drugs. And I think a lot more.

Frank is a big guy. About six feet two inches and two hundred pounds. He has a tough veneer, but when the DCFS lawyer finished, Frank was sobbing. I took him from the room and tried my best to console him. When he settled down I asked what made him upset. The reference to drugs? Sex? Crime? Suing to get his money?

Frank shook his head but could not or would not articulate. That night, as I held my now sleeping son and stroked his head, I knew. I knew that from the time he was Joey's age he had cried and wept and pleaded until he was empty. And what about those who should have heard his cries, whom we pay to hear his cries, and should have helped? They called him a junkie, a whore.

I went back to bed but could not sleep. I got up, went to my desk, and wrote essentially what you have just read. The next day I sent it to the *Chicago Tribune*. A few days later an editor phoned. He liked the article and wanted to publish it. But he wanted a DCFS response. I agreed.

Several days later I was told that the director of DCFS and several of his top aides would attend the next conference with Judge Rovner. At the conference the officials were all smiles while their lawyer grimaced in the background.

Would I consider settling?

Of course.

Then the director turned to the judge. They would give Frank a very substantial sum, more than the private agency. But there were two stipulations. First, I could never publish exactly what the settlement was. Second, I had to withdraw the article from the *Tribune*. I accepted.

The agency, like any government bureaucracy, would not mind years of litigation and even a substantial adverse judgment. After all, taxpayers would support both the litigation and the judgment. But one word of adverse publicity? That strikes at the heart and soul of the bureaucracy and cannot be tolerated. Confidences must be protected.

6

NEW REALITIES

Child welfare reformers founded our juvenile justice apparatus almost a hundred years ago. At the time, society assumed
that parents could assault, abuse, and ignore their children
pretty much as they could their personal property. Adolescents who stole or assaulted were either cut loose by judges
unwilling to lock them up with hardened adults, or tossed into
prisons by judges who didn't care what happened to them
there. Parents overwhelmed by the hand the fates had dealt
them drank, gambled, and fought. Not infrequently, one of
them, usually the father, abandoned the family. There being
no welfare, the remaining parent could not keep the family together. So thousands of half-orphans were crammed into al-

ready overflowing orphanages, most of them run by religious charities on nickels and dimes.

Faced with this late-nineteenth-century reality, caring leaders devised a juvenile or family court structure in an attempt to ameliorate these problems in a manner both acceptable and reasonable to society. In most cases parents would not be criminally punished for abusing their children. But society, acting through the courts, would step in to protect children who were broken or fragile and who were threatened because of their parents' actions. Young criminals, then called delinquents, would be segregated from older felons both in court and in prison. Religious charities continued to provide most of the services for both children and their families but could receive those government funds that followed a ward of the state. Welfare was not yet available to help women who had been widowed or whose husbands had abandoned them, but reformers kept pushing. Soon the government gave meager support to widows with small children but not to children whose fathers had abandoned the family. A couple of decades later, modest welfare programs were instituted by the Franklin D. Roosevelt administration to assist poor children living with a single parent.

Umberto Eco, the Italian novelist, tells the story of Italy's last king, Vittorio Emanuele III, who was once escorted through an art museum by a fawning curator. The king stood in front of a landscape depicting a quaint village nestled beside a river in a lush valley. Emanuele was apparently more interested in affairs of state than affairs of art, for after considering the picture for several minutes he turned to the curator and asked how many people lived in the village.

At least at one level the king considered the painting a living document rather than a landscape forever frozen by the artist's conception of it at one point in time. Real life is just the opposite, more like the painting. Government responds to a problem or crisis by inventing a solution, at times a bureaucratic one. Years or decades later, the precipitating causes of the problem or the nature of the crisis may have changed. But the government/bureaucratic solution usually remains frozen at its conception.

The juvenile justice and child welfare systems remain generally frozen in two particular eras, the first one in the late nineteenth and early twentieth centuries, when the Juvenile Court was founded, and the second in the early 1970s, when strict due process considerations invaded the juvenile courts. Now, in the late twentieth century, a new reality has settled in, but the lawyers, judges, child welfare social workers, and academics who run and influence the child welfare and juvenile justice systems continue to slug along as if it were 1899, or at least 1970.

Things have indeed changed since society's leaders faced the problems of the 1890s. In just the last fifteen years the landscape has been significantly altered. According to Department of Health and Human Services statistics from September 1996, the number of maltreated children has increased from 625,000 in 1980 to 1.5 million in 1993. To be more specific, in 1980 there were 42,900 sexual abuse cases nationally; in 1993 that number had leaped to 217,700—or from .7 per thousand children in the population to 3.2 per thousand. General abuse cases increased from 337,000 in 1980 to 743,200 in 1993, or from 5.3 per thousand to 11.1

per thousand. The increase of very seriously abused children is even more troubling, from 143,300 in 1986 to 569,900 just seven years later, or from 2.3 to 8.5 per thousand children. Neglect cases increased from 315,000 to 879,000.

Nationally the number of children in the custody of our child welfare agencies has doubled, from about 250,000 in 1983 to about half a million today. In Cook County the number has increased even more dramatically: between 1983 and 1986 it remained relatively constant at about 8,000 children in the custody of DCFS, but today the figure is over 40,000.

A new reality has settled in, but the lawyers, judges, child welfare bureaucrats, and academics who run and influence the child welfare and juvenile justice systems continue to operate according to old notions. If anything, parents seem to have greater property rights over their children, at least in Juvenile Court. And while parents are occasionally prosecuted for assaulting their children, it is a rare and newsworthy exception. The child welfare establishment still considers itself the ultimate *parens patriae*, the kindly parent, who will in most cases stabilize dysfunctional families.

In the late sixties and early seventies, lawyers like myself championed the due process revolution in Juvenile Court. We argued that informal, lawyerless proceedings deprived salvageable parents of their children. Adding insult to injury, the state often sinned against the children worse than their parents had. Over the next several decades, judges having rap sessions with social workers and families were replaced by judges in black robes on elevated benches hearing out lawyers representing the state, the child welfare agency, the parents, and the child. Not infrequently, at least four lawyers appear before a Juvenile Court judge in Cook County: the state's attorney prosecuting the abuse case, our office representing the child's interest, the public defender representing the parent, and a lawyer representing the child welfare agency. Occasionally a conflict between the parents means yet another taxpayer-supported lawyer.

All this due process has advanced the cause of some children, perhaps even their families. But too often protracted, formal, and expensive proceedings have robbed children of precious time, delayed the inevitable, and, worse, sometimes impeded an expeditious and just conclusion. I suppose, on the plus side, they have provided employment for thousands of lawyers, judges, court reporters, bailiffs, and janitorial staff who clean up after everyone leaves the courtroom.

More due process and lawyering were needed in a court system that prohibited parental abuse but ignored systemic government neglect that children often suffered when they became wards of the state. But today we must decide whether this intensive lawyering and judging stand in the way of progress. Couldn't highly motivated and trained social workers and caseworkers operating in the community more effectively and more quickly provide services to many children and families, at less expense to the taxpayers?

Yet the trend is for even more due process and more lawyering. The due process revolution has reached a point of being no longer family or child friendly but lawyer, judge, and bureaucrat friendly. Middle-class judges and lawyers trained in rigorous Socratic reasoning are now asked to resolve child-rearing problems of, for the most part, uneducated, frequently unemployed and unemployable women on welfare who are raising fatherless children. Juvenile court judges now grapple with many problems that could be more readily resolved by experienced, professional social workers.

It's time to take a fresh look at abuse and neglect. We no longer have the resources to grapple with the numbers of children pouring into and remaining in substitute care. More important, judges, hearing officers, court reporters, sheriffs, prosecutors, and lawyers for parents and children do not ensure that family-related problems of child abuse will be resolved.

I suggest the following changes.

(1) The juvenile courts now have two broad responsibilities in abuse and neglect cases. First the judge must determine whether the parents have abused the child. Once this decision has been made, the judge decides what the disposition should be. In most cases the court turns the family over to a child welfare agency to provide substitute care for the child and services for the parents so that the child can be returned to the family as quickly as possible. I believe that many of these responsibilities can be removed from the court and placed solely within the social work and child welfare systems.

(2) Classifications of abuse and neglect should be replaced by three separate categories of Abuse—I, II, and III.

(3) Child welfare bureaucracies should be broken into two separate agencies. One agency would consist of master's-degreed social workers, highly experienced caseworkers, registered nurses, and law enforcement officers, all responsible for the investigation of child abuse. If they determined there was abuse or neglect, they would have the option of referring

the case to court or working with the family in the community. The second agency would be responsible for providing services to families and children either pursuant to court order or through voluntary arrangements entered into by the initial agency and the parents.

(4) The Juvenile Court should be replaced by a *parens patriae* court which would consider all issues of individuals disabled either by age or mental processes.

1. THE SOCIAL WORK AND CHILD WELFARE SYSTEMS SHOULD
   BE GIVEN MORE RESPONSIBILITIES

At the front end of the system, most abuse and neglect cases are brought to court by state or local child welfare agencies. In at least half these cases, the parent or parents agree to temporary custody. The court then appoints the child welfare agency to act as temporary custodian, and the agency enlists a relative, usually a grandmother, aunt, or cousin to become the foster parent. Although the court may set a visitation schedule, informal visits probably occur, more or less supervised by the relative. At the end of this process, the court frequently sends the children home under a court order. The matter comes back to court anywhere between one and five times for the court to determine how the family is doing.

Before the due process revolution, families and extended families, frequently assisted by social workers, made these kinds of arrangements informally. A relative would step in and either temporarily or permanently raise the child of someone who was incapable of doing so. As due process gained favor, lawyers like myself argued that the child welfare community was an inappropriate vehicle to ensure due process, that the juvenile justice system must step in to regulate these familial arrangements.

As it turns out, courts are a cumbersome apparatus for the working out of family problems. For instance, a mother who loses her children may get her act together quickly enough to get them back; but because the next court date is so distant, she becomes discouraged and relapses into drugs, thus losing any chance she has to reclaim her children. When she finally does get to court, the parties may not have enough time to deal with her situation adequately, so the matter is continued. Again she fails to get her children back, causing problems for the children as well as for herself.

The legal system, particularly the judicial legal system, is like major surgery: it should not be used unless absolutely necessary and unless there is no alternative. Lawyers and judges are not trained to deal with the nuances of family life, particularly of the kinds of families we deal with. In most cases they are underclass families with reality-based depression and a great deal of substance abuse.

Similarly, at the back end of the system, once a judge decides that the family can be trusted to take care of a child, there is no reason for the court to continue monitoring. In most cases I would terminate all court involvement once the children are returned to the parents. At this point the monitoring of the family is a social work function. If the social workers ultimately determine that the family is not doing its job, they can either deal with it themselves or refer it back to court.

Over the past several decades the child welfare community has been marginalized by juvenile courts. The social work profession has been forced to play an increasingly diminished role, often in deference to young and inexperienced lawyers. Turning decision-making back to social workers should strengthen that profession and perhaps enable it once again to attract strong, talented, decent young people who now choose other professions.

2. CLASSIFICATIONS OF ABUSE AND NEGLECT SHOULD BE REPLACED BY THREE SEPARATE CATEGORIES OF ABUSE—I, II, AND III

Under the current system, when a court determines that a child has been abused or neglected, the child may be removed from the home. Visitation, return home, and other parental rights are then premised upon the parents' reform, irrespective of the nature of the abuse or neglect. The umbrella of abuse and neglect is wide. Abuse encompasses the slapping or whipping of a child—but also battering the kid to a pulp, and all the gradations of physical abuse in between. Sexual abuse covers cases where parents sexually assault the children or allow paramours and others to do so. But it also includes situations in which a parent may be so drugged or depressed that she does not know the child is being taken advantage of—often by a paramour or drug supplier. (In about half these cases, the mother throws the pervert out when she discovers the abuse. But too often the mother refuses to admit the abuse, thus sacrificing her child's safety and mental health for the relationship she has with the jerk.)

Neglect includes parents who take money meant for their kids and spend it on drugs, leaving their kids to sleep on urine-soaked mattresses, seldom attend school, live in roach-

and rat-infested heatless dumps, and raise themselves. But it can also include a mother suffering reality-based depression because at twenty-two she realizes that with four fatherless children and an eighth-grade education, her future is in the past.

Once a court finds that a parent has abused or neglected a child, most state laws (as dictated by the federal government) give that parent a certain period of time to demonstrate "reasonable efforts" toward getting the child back. According to federal guidelines, the state must also offer services to the parent to allow him or her to make these reasonable efforts.

The most abusive parents are often shrewd enough to get their lives together in order to convince a judge. But not infrequently, because of the pressures of underclass life, parents who commit minimal abuse never right themselves to the satisfaction of the court or social workers. Hence they never get their children back, or don't get them back quickly. Even worse, some parents demonstrate just enough concern to prevent a termination of their rights but not enough to regain custody of their children, who then languish for years in a frequently unkind child welfare system.

If the state wishes to terminate a parent's rights and allow the child to be placed for adoption, the state must show by clear and convincing evidence that the parent has not made reasonable efforts to recover the child despite the offer of services. Termination can be defeated in many cases, even when the parent has made no reasonable efforts, if the state has failed to provide an effective offer of services to help the parent.

For instance, we are currently involved in a case of a

young boy named Jamale born in September 1989 with drugs in his system. His mother has never been part of his life. His father has been in prison for most of Jamale's seven years, but even during his time outside, the father has visited Jamale only sporadically. Now the father is back in prison, and the state is attempting to terminate his parental rights. He has argued successfully, however, that the child welfare bureaucracy has not provided him with services to enable him to make reasonable efforts to gain custody of his son.

It is sensible to give a parent time to try to overcome the situation that brought his child into the system. It is equally sensible for the state to provide services to help the parent make this effort. But it is ludicrous to argue that the state must track down the parent to offer these services. The burden should be on the parent to come forward and seek the services from the state. The present law in effect makes the state equally responsible and equally culpable with the parent for abuse and neglect of the child.

Nor does the state's role as provider of helpful services guarantee success. In December 1996 a four-year-old child was pummeled to death in Illinois allegedly by his mother. The child had been born with drugs in his system. The mother had two older children, neither of whom ever received any attention from her. Both were in the child welfare system, and one was on her way to being adopted. Yet the system pursued the mother, trying to get her to accept services so she could get her third child back. She finally did when the child was a little over two years of age. Ultimately she got off drugs and cooperated with her counselors. The child was returned to her and was dead within three months. The mother was trying to tell us something for the first two years—that she did not want the child. But we in the system would not listen to her and forced the services upon her.

Some cases are so serious that we should move to terminate parents' rights immediately. Decisions should more closely mirror the reasons why the case came into the system. And many cases can be resolved by the child welfare community outside the due process straitjacket of a court system.

I would do away with the distinctions between abuse and neglect and create three new categories—Abuse I, Abuse II, and Abuse III. Abuse I would include most cases of sexual abuse, torture, and the murder of a sibling. I would also include in this category cases of long-standing and irreversible serious mental illness and severe retardation. Although the parents are not at fault in such cases, neither are they usually equipped to raise the children.

All Abuse I cases would be directed toward fast-track termination of parental rights. If the court finds a parent guilty of Abuse I, parental rights should be terminated within six months unless contrary to the child's best interest.

Abuse II would include most cases of serious physical abuse, long-standing neglect, and abandonment, such as parents leaving children unsupervised and without food for weeks at a time. Abuse II would also include all cases where parents have serious and long-standing drug or alcohol problems that have caused them to abuse or neglect their children. In Abuse II cases the court would give the parents fifteen months to demonstrate that the behavior that caused them to lose their children will not be repeated. With limited exceptions, if they did not the state would immediately move to terminate parental rights and place children for adoption. The state should offer the parents help in these cases, but failure to do so would not relieve a parent of the obligation to develop minimal parenting skills.

Abuse III could include as many as a third of the cases we now deal with in our juvenile courts. Now, when overwhelmed (not evil) parents crumble under the weight of underclass life, turn to drugs, and leave their kids to raise themselves, lawyers are appointed for the parents and most often for the children. The state prosecutes the parents, and usually they agree that at least temporarily they are not capable of taking care of the children. The children are then made wards of the state which, in most cases today, places them with a relative.

I would give the child welfare bureaucracy the choice of referring Abuse III cases to court; leaving the children at home and providing family preservation services; or encouraging the parents voluntarily to give up their children to a relative in exchange for services for up to six months. In these cases the state would have a contractual obligation to provide services.

Family preservation advocates argue that it is less expensive for the taxpayer and more beneficial to the child and the family to provide the parents with services that may include intensive social work, counseling, homemakers, and cash incentives. But under this system many parents, particularly those charged with serious abuse, have no incentive to turn their lives around. Inexperienced caseworkers often cannot distinguish between serious abuse and neglect and what is chiefly the result of poverty and lack of community support.

Recent studies seem to confirm that family preservation has failed in part because workers provide services to inappropriate families. Under my proposed system, social workers would have guidelines because family preservation would be available only in Abuse III cases. And only social workers with at least a master's degree in social work or other experienced caseworkers would deal with Abuse III cases.

Under this Abuse III category, if the parents agreed to voluntary placement of their children, the state child welfare agency would be obliged to provide services to help the parents overcome their problems. At the same time the parents would have generous unsupervised visitation rights with their children. Since the parents had made the decision for voluntary placement, they would clearly be motivated to recover their children quickly. In most cases I would expect that the children could be returned in less than six months. But if at the end of six months the parents still had not taken advantage of available services, the case would be screened into court.

3. CHILD WELFARE BUREAUCRACIES SHOULD BE BROKEN INTO TWO SEPARATE AGENCIES

In all but a few U.S. jurisdictions, the state or local child welfare agency investigates allegations of child abuse and neglect, provides family preservation services, refers appropriate cases to court, and, pursuant to court order, provides guardianship services which may include foster or residential care. The agency may provide any of these services directly or by contract with private agencies.

Thus child welfare agencies generally have three responsibilities: (1) investigate child abuse and refer appropriate cases to court; (2) provide substitute care; and (3) work with parents to help put their families together again. This too broad mandate sets the stage for the system's well-publicized failures. The mandates themselves are often conflicting. And the investigation and reporting of child abuse is too important to be left to the discretion of only the social work community. Child welfare's broad mandate has no doubt given rise to poor decision-making such as we often see in family preservation. And it should come as no surprise that parents whose children are taken by a child welfare agency do not exactly trust the agency's services.

Government child welfare bureaucracies should be broken up to reflect their missions. One agency, consisting of master's-degreed social workers, nurses, and law enforcement officers would be responsible for child protection. The second agency would be responsible for providing services for families and substitute care for children.

The child protective agency would classify a case as Abuse I, II or III, in some cases by working with the prosecuting authority. If it decided on Abuse III family preservation, the agency would then refer the family to the service providing agency. If the case were referred to court, the service providing agency would work with the court to provide substitute care for the children and/or services for the parents.

4. THE JUVENILE COURT SHOULD BE REPLACED BY A *PARENS PATRIAE* COURT

Juvenile courts are a relatively recent codification of the state's *parens patriae* responsibility. For centuries governments have exercised this power to protect those unable to care for themselves, including children and the mentally disabled. Abused or neglected children certainly need this protection. Some delinquents do as well. At the turn of the century it made sense to deal with adolescent window breakers and apple stealers together. Today a new underclass reality has altered the landscape, but the child welfare establishment and the government refuse to adapt or even to admit that some of our initial approaches no longer work.

I would do away with the juvenile court concept and set up a *parens patriae* court to enforce the state's responsibility to protect those unable to protect themselves. This court's umbrella would cover abused and neglected children, an increasing number of frail elderly, and the mentally disabled and impaired. In addition to providing guardianship and mental health services, the court should logically include the prosecution of miscreants who take advantage of a person's frailties to exploit him physically, sexually, or financially.

Today's reality dictates that adolescent criminals—who used to be known as juvenile delinquents—have little in common with abused children. Adolescent criminals should have their cases tried as a discrete part of the criminal justice system. The logic of mixing delinquents and abused infants and toddlers in one court may once have made sense, but that time has long since passed. Delinquency courts should be a juvenile division of the criminal justice system. A delinquency court judge would still employ the state's *parens patriae* power to protect the minor by providing services or placing him or her in a juvenile facility. In rare but appropriate cases an adolescent would be prosecuted and treated as an adult. But just because a child who commits a criminal act is treated differently from an adult does not mean that the case should not be heard in a juvenile division of the criminal justice system.

The focus of a *parens patriae* court would be much broader than what the juvenile courts now consider. The jurisdiction of a *parens patriae* court would include child abuse and neglect cases, cases involving elderly individuals who require guardianship because of Alzheimer's and organic brain disease, and cases of individuals who need commitment because of mental illness or a developmental disability. The domestic relations division might refer a complex child custody case. The court would also hear criminal cases in which an individual is charged with taking advantage of a person's disability or youth to commit a crime against that individual. Thus this court would hear criminal cases in which individuals, including parents, are charged with sexual or physical assault of children, or financial or physical exploitation of the elderly or the mentally disabled.

With this broader mandate, intelligent and motivated judges would wish to be assigned to the *parens patriae* court. They would be trained specifically to deal with *parens patriae* issues. And, though the jurisdiction of the *parens patriae* court would be much broader than the Juvenile Court, its focus would be narrower. The focus of the present Juvenile Court is sloppily broad, including adolescents who commit criminal acts and infants who are abused by their parents. The focus of a *parens patriae* court would be on children unable to protect themselves because they are at the mercy of their parents, and, at the other end of the spectrum, on individuals who because of age-related debility or mental illness are unable to protect themselves.

Could Sears and Wards compete against upstarts such as Walmart or Target using the same distribution and marketing techniques today that they employed in 1900 or 1970? The answer is obvious. But government, and specifically the courts and social service agencies, have a monopoly on the distribution and marketing of their services. Societal problems that prompted the creation of governmental responses may have disappeared or changed radically, but the government programs continue to battle dragons of the past. Government unions add to the inertia, making job security and seniority promotion, not services to clients, the main focus of the bureaucracy. The juvenile courts and the child welfare system must learn to adapt quickly and flexibly to the challenges of an evolving society.

7

WRONG RACE, WRONG PLACE

In the first half of this century, white racism and white fear prevented the placement of black children in Caucasian homes. Then, in the 1960s, as the civil rights movement gathered steam, more and more African-American children found their way into white foster and adoptive homes. But a counter-revolution, spawned mostly by a vocal minority of black social workers, has abruptly reversed this trend. These folks argue that "transracial" placement of black children cuts them off from their cultural roots and ultimately harms both

them and black American society. The social service bureaucracies have caved in to these notions, and transracial placement has become increasingly rare. In my judgment, the lives
of thousands of black children have been chewed up and spit
out because of a stupid, shortsighted policy.

I had just returned from vacation in the late summer of 1994
when Robert got it. Robert, like my two sons, had not yet
reached puberty. At age eleven he was about sixteen months
younger than my twelve-year-old and about the same height
as my nine-year-old, four feet six inches tall. One of my
lawyers had represented Robert in court. She called him a little "pumpkin," said he was cuddly.

Robert wasn't your typical eleven-year-old—at least I
hope not. He was pretty much a sociopath by his third birthday, perhaps earlier.

Robert caught his first bad break when he was born. His
mother had her first child, an older brother, when she was fifteen. She herself had been born to a teenage mother. Robert's
mom was the third of ten children by four different fathers;
she never knew her own.

Despite being a cuddly pumpkin, Robert wasn't the type
of child you'd like your own kids playing with. He began running with the Black Disciples gang on Chicago's South Side
when he was eight. At nine he was arrested for attempted
armed robbery. When he was ten his probation officer told the
judge that "Robert is a heavy duty gangbanger. He has the
worst attendance record. . . . He missed 93 days of school this
year." (This was about six weeks before the end of the school
year.) Robert was the third born; by the time his mother was

nineteen, she had four children and was entrenched in the AFDC, food-stamp, underclass welfare world. And things were not going well for Robert and his brothers and sisters.

In 1984 Robert's mother was investigated and cited for neglect by the state child protection agency for failing to follow doctor's orders in treating Robert's two-year-old brother. This child ultimately went blind. Less than a year later Robert was admitted to Jackson Park Hospital with scratch marks on his neck and bruises on his arms and torso. About a year later, in January 1986, Robert's sixteen-month-old sister suffered second- and third-degree burns on her vagina, buttocks, and thighs. The child had just happened to rub up against the radiator in the wrong way, mom explained.

The emergency room physicians said it couldn't have occurred that way, but the DCFS worker referred the mother to parenting classes. A week later, before these classes started, a neighbor dialed 911 because mom had disappeared in the morning, leaving the sixteen-month-old, two-year-old Robert, and his three-year-old blind brother in the care of a five-year-old brother. The neighbors told the police that "mother leaves children alone on a daily basis—only returning late at night."

On this occasion the police had all children examined at the hospital. It turned out that Robert had linear ("cord-like") marks on his abdomen and legs. He also had "cigarette-like burns on the back of neck and on lower right shoulder blade; four healing cigarette-like burns on buttocks." His mother later said the burns were really chicken pox scars, but she didn't explain how both of his brothers had similar "cigarette-like burns." Nor did she explain how four years later, in 1990, after having several more kids, one of them was examined for "cigarette-like burns" on his "forearm, behind his ear, on his wrist and on his right calf." That child also had "multiple scars on his upper and lower back."

Some of the professionals who looked at the family situation concluded that the placement of the children with the maternal grandmother was not a good idea. The children needed a warm and nurturing environment—something they had never known—if they were to get a decent education and eventually be able to take care of themselves. One professional recommended that the children be placed together in the same home, or at least in warm and nurturing foster homes, until the mother had demonstrated she was able to care for her children. And if the mother did not get her act together in eighteen months, this report declared, the children should be placed for adoption outside their nuclear or extended family.

The state placed Robert, now not quite three years of age, in a hospital for evaluation. When the child abuse worker said something that angered the little boy, he grabbed a toy knife and rushed the woman. "Fuck you, you bitch," he cried, sticking the rubber blade into the worker's arm. "I'm gonna cut you."

The state's child welfare bureaucracy soon became the guardian of Robert and his siblings. Ignoring the professionals, it placed the four children with grandma. Over the next several years, while mom had three more children, it pursued her with services which she failed to take advantage of, probably because of her drug dependency. And grandma wasn't exactly a kindly white-haired lady making apple pies and singing lullabies from a rocking chair. She was in her early thirties when Robert's mom started having babies, and she herself had children Robert's age.

Granny lived in a decent black working-class community. Some of her neighbors didn't like her, her ten children and thirty grandchildren who from time to time inhabited her three-bedroom home. A few initiated an unsuccessful petition drive to get rid of her and the family. As Robert grew older, he began to get into trouble, which shouldn't have surprised anyone. By age eleven he had accumulated about twenty arrests, including some for arson, robbery, theft, and burglary.

After an attempted armed robbery charge, Robert was again evaluated. Not surprisingly, the therapist wrote that "he approaches the world with much wariness and hypervigilance; he is overly suspicious. He is caught up in a never ending cycle of emotional overload and acting out. His anger is so great that his perception of the world is grossly distorted and inaccurate." Later she wrote that although Robert was at the lower end of the normal IQ scale, he "is unable to read, and as such, the paper and pencil questionnaires had to be read to him." Robert could not read because he had failed to go to school—no one had gotten him there or insisted he get there.

Shavon, a pleasant fourteen-year-old girl about to start high school, lived around the corner from Robert. On Sunday, August 28, 1994, she left a family barbecue to walk a friend home. At the same time Robert's gang apparently sent him on a mission, probably caused by a personal insult or a drug deal gone bad. The eleven-year-old began blasting away with his .9 mm automatic at a group of boys playing football. One of the bullets hit a fifteen-year-old child in the hand. Another found Shavon's head, killing her instantly.

For the next several days, Chicago police went on a highly publicized boy hunt, sealing Robert's fate. His buddies in the gang could never let him live to finger them. So four days after Shavon was murdered, two Black Disciples took Robert for a walk under a deserted underpass and shot him in the back of his head.

Robert's mother who, with her additional children, was in and out of grandma's house, declared Robert was misunderstood and was just "an average 11 year old." Grandma threw herself on the coffin and blamed the cops, the media, the schools, and the courts for Robert's problems. His neighbors were less charitable. "Nobody didn't like that boy. Nobody gonna miss him," one boy told a *Time* magazine reporter.

Since the Black Disciples had the lack of foresight to send eleven-year-old Robert on his mission and to his death during the late summer media doldrums, Robert's story made the national and even the international wires. Myself, I couldn't figure out what all the hullabaloo was about. Robert had been tracked to a miserable destiny from birth. He would sooner or later have killed or be killed or die while serving life sentences several years at a time. Since it was sooner, and since he was both a killer and a victim, his mug shot appeared in *People*. Robert's family had no photo of him, so they had to use the police mug shot at his coffin.

A few days after Robert was executed, I reviewed the file of a fifteen-year-old boy who had been shot and killed at the Robert Taylor Homes, a mammoth Chicago housing project, during a gang shoot-out. This boy's background was the same as Robert's and that of thousands of others my office sees every year—teenage mother, lots of siblings fathered by lots of men, no real dads, AFDC and Juvenile Court, first for being neglected, then for delinquency. This fifteen-year-old boy didn't make the national or international wires. He didn't even make the local ones, or even the obituary page. Reporters, like the rest of us, have come to expect that fifteen-year-old black kids will kill or be killed, or end up dead or wounded or in jail.

Robert was fast-tracked to an early doom, but we had several opportunities to derail him and failed. Recall that when he was not yet three, professionals recognized that his mother probably was incapable of caring for her children. They suggested giving her eighteen months and then terminating her rights. They also recommended placing Robert and his siblings in a nurturing foster home or homes, not with grandma. But the advice was ignored. Why did the child welfare professionals and the courts pay for and then not heed what in hindsight was excellent advice?

The child welfare response would be that this was an optimum recommendation but not necessarily practical. Despite being a drug addict, the mother showed hints of capability. Indeed, she had had additional children whom—with state support and services—she had raised with moderate success. And while the therapist wasn't exactly enamored with grandma's potential to raise children, she *was* family. Placing the children with her cushioned the blow of separation from their mother. By living with grandma, the children would have continued access to their mother, albeit in a relatively protected atmosphere. Besides, we don't have enough kind, loving, and nurturing foster homes for children without relatives who can accept them.

Wasted

Of course children are better off with a reformed parent, assuming the parent quickly demonstrates a willingness to reform. And children *should* be placed with relatives where possible. Relative foster care has saved the child welfare system over the past dozen years or so. In Illinois, for instance, relatives now provide approximately 60 percent of all substitute care. But sometimes the relatives aren't much better than the parents. Often the parent has visited problems upon the children which he or she inherited from his or her own parents. Placing the child with the relative increases the chances that the child will be further harmed by a grandma or aunt who is as dysfunctional as the mother or father.

But the bottom line, welfare advocates argue, is the lack of adequate foster homes. Given their formula for placing children, they are right. That's because their formula includes roadblocks which prevent the neediest children from being united with a potential pool of foster and adoptive parents. The foster and adoptive parents are white, and the kids needing services are black.

If this were the forties or fifties, to deny these children foster placement for such a reason would be racist and unconstitutional. But in the politically correct nineties, the placement of black children into white homes is considered racist. A vocal and substantial minority of social workers have intimidated those who know better, and most social workers have caved in on the issue for fear of being branded racist.

In 1994 an Illinois state senator asked the Illinois chapter of the National Association of Social Workers to offer a point-counterpoint article in its newsletter on the issue of transracial adoption. The social workers, however, felt "this issue is too controversial for NASW...." At a meeting set up in part to respond to concerns of the state senator, a Ph.D. social worker pointed out that transracial placements had been going on since 1954 and had reached a peak in 1972, when black social workers came out heavily against it. He argued that African-American children are the greatest resource of the African-American community and that transracial adoption was stripping this resource from that community. The chairperson of the Chicago chapter of the National Association of Black Social Workers, an adoption worker with DCFS, declared that transracial adoption "is not a good alternative for African-American children in the child welfare system." Both said that agencies should do a better job of recruiting African-American foster parents and adoptive parents.

Both the private and public sectors have been hustling over the past decade to develop African-American foster and adoptive homes. But while increasing joblessness, misery, and drug addiction in the underclass have led to increasing numbers of black children needing placement, the percentage of African Americans in the population remains relatively constant. Placing a black child in an African-American foster or adoptive home, like family preservation, makes sense on paper. But it places a burden on middle-class African-American families that we do not place on middle-class white families. Most important, the resource simply is not there.

For instance, in Cook County approximately 88 percent of the 40,000 children now in DCFS custody are African-American while only about one-third of Cook County's residents are black. In 1995 Illinois had 39,689 African-American, 10,186 white, and 2,191 Hispanic children in state custody. The population totals are skewed against black kids. Approximately 9 million whites live in Illinois but only 1.7 million blacks and 900,000 Hispanics. To put it another way, for every white child in the custody of the state, there are about 900 other white people of all ages not in DCFS custody. For every Hispanic kid in the child welfare system in Illinois, there are 400 Hispanic people not in child welfare custody. But for every black child in state custody because of abuse or neglect, only 43 other black men, women, and children are not in state child welfare custody.

DCFS uses several temporary shelters for infants awaiting placement. When I go to the temporary shelter in Cook County, I rarely see a white face. In December 1994, at one of the larger temporary shelters, DCFS had placed 329 children between the ages of one and three. Of these, 300 were African-American, 19 white, and 7 Hispanic. (In three cases the child's race was not given in the data.) The figures were worse for children remaining at the shelter more than three months—67 black, 3 white, and 3 Hispanic. Of those in the shelter more than 6 months awaiting placement, 70 were black, 2 white, and 3 Hispanic. And of those still at the shelter awaiting placement after twelve months, 28 were African-American while none were white or Hispanic.

This particular shelter happens to be quite well run and has hundreds of volunteers who regularly hold and cuddle the infants and toddlers. Nevertheless an institution simply cannot provide the constant warmth and attention that an infant needs and deserves. Yet black kids languish in a shelter for want of available black foster care while thousands of white homes go unused. Ah, but it's okay, since at least they are not in honky foster care, being held and cooed at at three in the morning, where their presence would be stripping the African-American community of a valuable resource. Well-meaning child advocates, black and white, desperately want to pretend that reality is different from what it is. In 1994, when Congress debated a relatively weak bill mandating some form of transracial adoption, the NAACP, the National Association of Black Social Workers, the Children's Defense Fund, and the Child Welfare League of America all argued for policies promoting "minority parents for minority children," or same-race adoption.

But reality around the nation is the same as it is in Illinois. In 1995 the percentages of first-time admissions into foster care for five states, including Illinois, California, New York, Michigan, and Texas, showed that 35 percent of the children in foster care were white while 39 percent were black and 20 percent Hispanic. The combined population of these five states, according to the 1990 census, was approximately 63.2 million whites, 9.9 million blacks, and 15.2 million Hispanics.

In March 1995 California had 41,191 white children in state custody because of abuse or neglect, 39,486 black children, and 28,271 Hispanic children. California's population according to the 1990 census was approximately 20.5 million whites, 2.2 million blacks, and 7.6 million Hispanics. This would mean that for every abused white child in California custody, 500 whites of all ages were not similarly situated. For Hispanics the ratio was 1 to 271, but for blacks the ratio was only 1 to 56.

In New York state in 1993, 22 percent of all first admissions into the child welfare system were white, 45 percent black, and 15 percent Hispanic; the New York population had 13.3 million whites, 2.8 million blacks, and 2.2 million Hispanics. The figures are equally discouraging everywhere in the country. In March 1995, according to figures from the Department of Health and Human Services, Ohio had 11,173 whites in child welfare custody and 10,591 blacks. According to the 1990 census, there were 9.5 million whites living in the state as against 1.1 million blacks.

In 1994 Congress passed the Multi-Ethnic Placement Act in an effort to bring reason to racial gerrymandering in adoptive and foster placements. The law states that an agency or entity receiving federal financial assistance and involved in adoption or foster care placements may not discriminate on the basis of race, color, or national origin of the adoptive or foster parent or child involved. But the law gives agencies a major escape. It permits consideration of race, color, or national origin when an agency has made a narrowly tailored, individualized determination that a particular case requires such consideration in order to advance the best interest of the child in need of placement. In a particular case a good lawyer with vast resources might prove that an agency ignored the best interest of the child in order to prevent transracial placement. But in the majority of cases there are no lawyers, and no lawyers lurk nearby when an agency makes the initial determination not to place the child in a white foster home.

In May 1996 President Clinton signed another law attempting to bring sanity to transracial placement. This law permits agencies to place a black child with a qualified African-American family if one is available. But if one is not, the child is to be placed in the first available home irrespective of race. This law may inject some reason into placement considerations, but I wouldn't bet the mortgage on it. The 1994 act was just as strong, and, frankly, the 1996 act appears to be no more than political rhetoric. Besides, the child welfare establishment has pretty much ignored the 1994 act.

As President Clinton was signing the new transracial adoption bill, I was working on Jevonte's case. Jevonte was six weeks old when the Juvenile Court took him from his mother because of severe physical abuse, including a dislocated hip and a skull fracture. The Department of Children and Family Services placed him with a private agency, which cared for him in a special residential facility for infants for several months until he was healthy enough to live in foster care. In November 1995 DCFS began looking for a placement for the boy, specifically limiting its search to African-American families. At one point the caseworker contacted twenty-one black households, all of whom declined the child. Shortly thereafter a white foster mother, hearing of the child's plight, phoned and said her family was available. Later the foster mother showed up at the agency, but the caseworker discouraged her, charting in her notes that the "staff advised [the white foster mother] that the agency is still seeking same race placement as the possibility had not been exhausted and the return home goal had not been ruled out" (the last statement was untrue). Ultimately the agency found an African-American home with five other children under the age of five.

Agencies can cower behind the best interest of the child to avoid placing him in a white home. Meanwhile every statistic shows that black kids remain in the system longer, go through more foster homes and placements, and are adopted less frequently than their white counterparts. The lives of these black kids, like Robert, are sacrificed to conform to the philosophy of middle-class child advocates who speculate about the problems of the poor from the sanctity of academia or upscale restaurants but do not have to go through multiple foster placements or live several weeks each year in a shelter or end up as adolescents on the streets because they are a resource that must not be stripped from the African-American community.

I do understand the argument that because our society still thinks in racial and even racist terms, black children are better off raised within an African-American culture. But from a child's viewpoint, an "inferior" white home is better than many foster homes or the shelter or a granny like Robert's. And I've heard some of the other objections. A black child reared in a white or mostly white neighborhood could get called the "N" word or fail to get a date to the prom, or the foster parents might not know how to take care of the kid's hair. Sensitive adoptive parents can overcome these obstacles. Besides, a kid growing up in an all-black environment can have the "N" word spat at him too. And maybe the kid won't go to the prom. As with everything in life, the positives and negatives must be weighed.

This is not a black/white issue. Many African-Americans readily agree that children should be placed in the best available home irrespective of the race of the foster or adoptive home; a number of whites contend that the child's cultural background must be a foremost consideration. Randall

Kennedy, a black professor at Harvard Law School, has written: "There's simply no compelling reason to delay even briefly, for purpose of racial matching, placing parentless children in permanent homes. What parentless children need most are not 'white' parents or 'black' parents or 'yellow' parents but loving parents able to raise children in a nurturing environment."

8

ORPHANS IN A STORM

The word "orphanage" is not good coin among child welfare professionals. It has Dickensian connotations. Besides, there are few real orphans these days. "Residential care" is the modern equivalent. And the child welfare establishment generally finds residential care distasteful, arguing that children are better raised in their own families or in foster care. Two child advocates recently wrote in the *Chicago Tribune*: "Since the turn of the century, researchers have shown that warehousing children in orphanages causes them profound and irreparable harm. Instead of orphanages, the state should invest in policies that strengthen families and enable them to

162

eliminate the overwhelming stress of poverty from their lives."

In the late nineteenth century my grandmother, then a young child, immigrated from Northern Ireland with her parents. Ultimately the family settled in the Back of the Yards section of Chicago while her father worked in the stockyards. When she was fifteen the local bartender got to her, and my father was born nine months later. Shortly after that she married a guy who spent too much time at the local saloon and had four more children by him. When he wasn't drinking he was batting my grandma around, and when he wasn't abusing her he was taking it out on the kids, chiefly my father, who wasn't his. Ultimately he did everyone a favor by disappearing into the alcoholic underworld.

My grandma took in laundry at a dollar a day and raised the infant but, there being no welfare in those days, she could not handle the other four. They were shipped off to St. Mary's Training School (now called Maryville), an orphanage in what was then farmland northwest of Chicago. My dad, his two brothers, and a sister remained there for three years until Bill Murphy came along, married my grandmother, and adopted her children, including my dad. Together they had several more children.

But money was tight. Instead of going on to high school, when my dad left St. Mary's at age fourteen he went to work. When I was a kid, my dad worked in the stockyards and then drove a streetcar. He and his siblings would be surprised to learn that their three years at St. Mary's caused them "profound and irreparable harm." But somewhere he went wrong:

of the eight children he sired and nurtured to graduate degrees, four became lawyers.

The welfare system that was born in the 1930s, plus more reasoned family planning, soon diminished the number of orphans. Orphanages became part of a substitute-care system for abused and neglected children, particularly where foster care failed to work. But beginning in the sixties, child welfare reformers argued that orphanages ran counter to the idea of family preservation and thus were obsolete. Children were to be kept with their parents or placed in foster care. The child advocates writing in the *Tribune* declared that rather than removing children from their parents, "we need to prevent abuse and neglect by strengthening families. Illinois families need investment in education, training, job development and creation, the earned income tax credit and subsidized, quality child care. And they need workplace policies that accommodate the needs of parents." The dean of the Columbia University School of Social Work contends that instead of spending money on orphanages, poor families would benefit more from counseling, parent training, and child welfare programs. "What we need are multi-service centers offering help to parents in high risk neighborhoods. . . ."

Too many child welfare types can't bring themselves to admit that there are cowards and bullies who are good at having babies but incapable of nurturing their children, with or without multiservice centers. They abuse their kids and ultimately lose them because down deep they never wanted them. And then what happens to the children?

Most kids will be returned home relatively quickly, or be adopted, or thrive in foster care. But thousands, usually the most damaged ones, careen through the system, through foster homes and shelters, back to foster care, back to the shelter, to a psychiatric hospital, to the streets, to shelters, back to the streets, perhaps to a foster home or two, and ultimately to the streets. Every move diminishes the child's self-esteem, which because of parental abuse and neglect is already in the sub-basement. And the more damaged the child becomes, the more he acts out to test unprepared foster parents, and the more he tests these foster parents the more they reject him, and the more damaged he becomes, the more he will act out to test future foster parents.

Shoving these children into additional foster homes or back into their own homes destroys them. Ultimately many just hit the streets and turn to male and female prostitution, drug abuse, and gangs. Many of the girls have babies and drop out of high school or junior high.

A few years ago the owner of a gay bar phoned. One of his employees, John, had abruptly stopped coming to work. After about a week, the owner, also a close friend of John's, became alarmed. Suspecting foul play, he called the police. They broke into John's flat where they discovered a body that the mid-August heat had pretty much destroyed. The police needed someone to identify the remains, and John's friend couldn't bring himself to do it. He phoned, explaining that John had often spoken about me. Would I go to the morgue to identify the corpse?

I thought I was in a grade B movie as I followed a beefy attendant down the dimly lit halls of the Cook County Morgue. "Tough to die like that," the attendant said.

I grunted.

"A friend?" he probed. Was I gay? A geek?

"I was his lawyer."

The attendant pulled back the sheet exposing a brown skull, looking like a rubber doll and bearing little resemblance to John. But the slightly deformed teeth were his. I stared at that hideous skull for what seemed like minutes, thinking of John. I had first met him when he was about ten and tied by full leather restraints to a bed in a state psychiatric center.

John wasn't crazy and didn't belong in a mental health facility. But the state child welfare agency, DCFS, relied upon psychiatric facilities for the care of children who were between placements or out of placements. John was a high-spirited, good-natured, but, as the psychiatrists say, "oppositional" kid. He squandered his foster home opportunities by being, well, high-spirited and oppositional. A slight ten-year-old with auburn hair and Huck Finn looks, he certainly did not require full leather restraints. But that was how the overextended, understaffed bureaucracy controlled kids' behavior in those days.

John and his brother Tom, a year younger, had come into the system when they were six and five. They had an abusive father and a passive mother who had a greater affinity for the bottle than for her children. They deserted, or maybe one died and the other just left. I forget. A grandmother tried coping with them for a year or so but gave up. The kids went through several foster homes and, briefly, a residential care facility together. Then DCFS split them up. John went through five or six additional foster homes. When DCFS ran out of places to put him, the agency dumped him and a couple of hundred other kids into state psychiatric facilities.

Neither the hospital nor the restraints did much to dampen John's spunky nature. I liked him instantly. Of course the restraints and the unneeded hospitalization angered me, and I sued to get him out. That took several months. Meanwhile I asked if I could take John from the facility on a couple of day excursions. Today the staff would legitimately worry about sexual exploitation, but in those days things were looser. Why not let him go? One fewer child for them to worry about. So I took John to see some pretty bad movies, and we visited some ice cream parlors. I even took him home once.

Ultimately we prevailed, and John was released to another foster home. I went on to other cases and other kids. Then, about three years later, I heard that DCFS had dumped about six hundred children in warehouse-type facilities in Texas. When I went down to get a firsthand look at these "camps," one of the first kids I encountered was John, who was then fourteen or fifteen. He liked the place because he didn't have to go to school. But there were downsides. Once he had killed a dog, and the staff had tied the dog's collar around John's neck and chained him to his bed with the dog's leash. They had also forced him to wear the dog's tail around his neck for a week.

We sued and brought the six hundred kids back from Texas. Just after that I left Legal Services and lost track of John. When he was about eighteen, he phoned. He was working as a male go-go dancer in a gay bar. He asked if I would come by to see him, sort of like a proud son would ask his father to see how he had succeeded. So I went. He did the bump and grind around a pole in one of those dimly lit joints where your shoes stick to the floor because of the grime and roaches race around a toilet that looks like it hasn't been flushed in a week and men masturbate each other in dark corners.

After that John sunk into the more violent, sadomasochistic side of the homosexual experience. He'd stop by my house or call every year or so for advice or a ten-dollar loan. After a while it dawned on me that it wasn't the advice he wanted, or even the money. He was a lonely, empty young man who craved companionship, a family, and a father. My pitifully few kind acts when he was a child made me family and father, albeit an insubstantial one.

The pathologists said he died of an autoerotic act. He tied one end of a rope around his neck and the other end to a closet door, and leaned forward while he masturbated. It's a way to get off big, but sometimes you lose consciousness and get off into the next world. I'm not sure it was an accident. Unconsciously John wanted to die for a long time. He believed he was worthless. It was a belief that John earned the hard way—through parents who couldn't or wouldn't become a mother and father; through a court system that saved him from parental neglect but then looked the other way as it entrusted him to state-sponsored abuse; through a child welfare system more concerned with the needs of the bureaucracy than those of an individual child; and finally through a lawyer who helped him out of tight spots and even gave him occasional attention but who wasn't there through the less obvious but more painful neglect of multiple placements, and who wasn't there for the kid as he became a young man.

Of course the reformers are correct. Children are much better raised by their own parents or by substitute parents. But what happens, as in John's case, when there are no available parents and when the child, for a variety of reasons, cannot be effectively raised by substitutes? In the world of child welfare, what is in a child's best interest is frequently limited to avoiding the worst. Both legal and social work academics turn their back on this reality. From the safe harbor of academia they preach of the need to be raised by good and kindly parents. In John's case they could rightly point out that he had been placed in residential care, if only briefly when he was six or seven, and again for a much longer period when he was a teenager. Neither experience seemed to help him. They could argue that the institutionalization in Texas may even have harmed him. It was a good example of a Dickensian facility.

But a bad orphanage does not obviate all residential care. Even academics and reformers would concede this, though they would argue that money spent on residential care would be better used to shore up marginal families. Again the question arises, what happens when the family is less than marginal and the kid cannot make it in foster care?

Children are happier and ultimately will be better adjusted if they live in a decent family environment. Even a marginal family, his own or a substitute, is usually better for a child than even the best residential facility. Orphanages, like just wars, should be employed only as a last resort, when no viable alternative exists. Even the best of them, with highly motivated, caring employees and live-in house parents, must rely on rigid rules and a formality that is at odds with a nurturing atmosphere in which a child usually prospers.

Nevertheless there are two stages in the life of an abused or neglected child in which residential care may be necessary and may even save him. John, for instance, could have benefited from residential care at both these stages.

Many young children, like John and his brother, are removed from their parents for good reason. But the children don't know this and suffer inner turmoil, believing they are the cause of the breakup. They may be only four or five, but they test every living situation and thus fail in foster care. Because the parents are so abusive or simply not there, the kids cannot go back home, so the child rotates from foster home to foster home, battering an already fragile self-esteem. At this moment a brief stint in residential care can stabilize very young children. Professionals working with children can bring them to the realization that the problem is not theirs and pave the way for future foster or adoptive care, even a return home.

But the child welfare establishment continues to resist residential care for philosophical and financial reasons. Philosophically their goal is still to preserve or reunify the family, and residential care is also more expensive than providing services to parents or, for that matter, foster care. Tax dollars, they argue, should be used to keep children at home, not for residential placement. From the point of view of the child welfare establishment, every dollar diverted to residential care is one less dollar for strengthening families.

But this argument overlooks the young children who have no real parents with whom they can live, and who will instead float among various foster homes. Too few facilities exist to help these children. One, in Oak Park, Illinois, Hephzibah, cares for about twenty children ranging in age between four and seven. These kids may go to the local school or be schooled on the grounds. They sleep in bedrooms with one or two other children and may remain at the facility for six to eighteen months while the staff tries to stabilize them and, in appropriate cases, help their parents toward reunification. The number of children requiring Hephzibah-like care is far greater than the available placements.

Virtually all young children deserve the stability and warmth of a nuclear family, where and if possible. Residential care for young children should be in the nature of therapeutic intervention to stabilize the child. But for adolescent children, the need for residential and group homes is desperate.

Even the best teenagers, living with the kindest, most understanding parents, experience widely fluctuating feelings of rebellion and turmoil. And what of a child like John, abandoned by his parents and a failure in foster care? What happens to him at age fourteen? Foster homes, state shelters, welfare hotels, gangs, drugs, the streets, back to foster care, ultimately prostitution and too early paternity.

The ages between fourteen and eighteen are rough years—for all concerned. The young person is neither a child nor an adult. Children in our system of substitute care have been rejected by their parents, either by physical or emotional abandonment or abuse or neglect. Too frequently they have failed in foster care. It is difficult enough for understanding parents to deal with their own adolescent children. A stranger getting paid several hundred dollars a month has an even tougher time. The kid tests the foster parent, and the foster parent frequently caves in.

Residential care for adolescents is unfortunately the only possible world for many teenagers. Most of the dedicated men and women who work in residential facilities view their jobs as vocations. They provide consistent professional care and security for insecure and unwanted children. Perhaps more important, they goad these kids into living up to their potential. The percentage of children living in residential care who graduate from high school and go on to college routinely is much higher than the similar numbers for foster care.

Most residential care facilities do not resemble the old-fashioned orphanage where, for instance, my dad lived. In those days, thirty or forty children may have lived in a dormitory and worked in the kitchen or bakery, on the farm, and so on. Indeed, the facility in which my father lived for three years is still in existence. Maryville is a good example of an excellent modern residential care facility. The children there, all adolescents, live in cottages, usually of eight kids each, run by live-in house parents. For the most part the children take their meals at the cottage and go to the local high school. The percentage of Maryville kids who graduate from high school and go on to college is much higher than anywhere else within the child welfare system.

Is residential care like family? No. Is it true family? Of

course not. Is it better than much of what the kids have seen? Absolutely.

The alternative to residential care is one that the child welfare system now uses for many of its adolescents: the streets.

9

IDEOLOGY AND REALITY

Edwin Markham, a nineteenth-century minister and poet, once viewed the famous painting by Jean François Millet of the French peasant tied to the soil—the way our fourth-world underclass is tied to housing projects and welfare checks. Markham wrote in part:

> Bowed by the weight of centuries he leans
> Upon his hoe and gazes on the ground,
> The emptiness of ages in his face,
> And on his back the burden of the world.
> Who made him dead to rapture and despair,
> A thing that grieves not and that never hopes,

Stolid and stunned, a brother to the ox? . . .
Is this the Thing the Lord God made and gave
To have dominion over sea and land;
To trace the stars and search the heavens for power;
To feel the passion of Eternity? . . .
Down all the stretch of Hell to its last gulf
There is no shape more terrible than this—
More tongued with censure of the world's blind greed—
More filled with signs and portents for the soul—
More fraught with danger to the universe.

I suspect that from that moment in the early dawn of man's history when our ancestors first began grappling with rudimentary tools, we have had an underclass. But never have we had one so mired in a sludge of ignorance, violence, and despair while surrounded by wealth, opportunity, and growth. And because our underclass has been created, and now in part sustained, by accidents of race, the situation is "fraught with danger" to our universe.

Politicians these days are rushing to the middle, but in underclass issues both the left and right have preconceived ideologies into which all problems must be neatly pigeonholed. The right would leave the underclass to its own devices; the left would relieve it of individual responsibility. Take, for instance, two matters I was involved with in the past year.

In 1995 a Cook County Criminal Court judge sentenced a congressman to four years in prison for a felony—having consensual sex with a sixteen-year-old high school student. The young woman was nineteen at the time of trial and was forced to testify.

A few months later Chicago police arrested thirty-four-year-old Salvador. His sister told the police that he had been living and having sex with twelve-year-old Maria. Maria's mom had brought her to Chicago from Mexico, and then had apparently returned to the south, leaving Salvador to care for her daughter.

Maria was barely thirteen years old and eight months pregnant when she appeared as a witness in a case charging Salvador with aggravated criminal sexual abuse. Since Maria was about six years short of adulthood, consent was not an issue; this was a simple case of statutory rape. And the case in which Maria testified was not an actual trial. It was a preliminary hearing to determine whether there was probable cause for Salvador to face a criminal trial. Since Maria was the only witness and the state had only to prove probable cause, the case was a no-brainer.

But it turned out not to be. Maria truthfully responded that she had consented to the sex, and the judge dismissed the case.*

About six months after Maria delivered her baby, one of the lawyers in my office attended the funeral of a five-year-old girl who had died of AIDS. Her seven-year-old sister is HIV positive, and her mother is pregnant again. I've seen

---

*After the judge's ruling, *Chicago Tribune* columnist Mike Royko blasted the judge and the state's attorney. The state's attorney ultimately went before a grand jury, which voted to indict Salvador. But by this time he had seen the writing on the wall and fled to Mexico.

worse cases. Take the experience of one woman whose boyfriend beat her newborn child to death in 1987. That baby was her seventh child; since then she has had six more, all born with cocaine in their systems, three with syphilis, and the last four born HIV positive. She abandoned three at the hospital. Her twelve living children reside in foster care. Society is paying at least a quarter of a million dollars a year to provide for them and her.

Abstinence from drugs and proper medical care could have resolved the drug and venereal disease exposure. And if the mother had taken AZT while pregnant, the chances are fairly good that her children could have been spared membership in the AIDS epidemic. Of course, had the mother listened to medical advice she may not have gotten pregnant with children she clearly didn't want. Drugs, alcohol, and underclass depression have destroyed this woman's mind; she should be more pitied than condemned. But her children have done nothing wrong and yet are sentenced to marginal, even brief, lives because of their mother's negligence. And society—that's us—are accomplices to that negligence.

A decade ago drug babies trickled into the child welfare system. Now they flood and overwhelm our juvenile courts so that in big-city jurisdictions we seldom act until the third or fourth child is born with drugs. A few years ago HIV infants began trickling in. While we are not yet in a flood stage, we are on the way. Yet, other than taking the damaged children away from the parents, we stand by helplessly while men and women, boys and girls, compromise the future potential of fetuses.

Because of these cases I wrote a piece for the *New York*

Times suggesting that a humane society should act to protect potential children from fetal abuse. I pointed out that while the mother had an absolute right to abort her fetus, I did not see how that right became a privilege to abuse a fetus who would soon be a child. Sterilization is out of the question for both legal and moral reasons, but society must devise a response to protect unborn children from parents whose irresponsible acts damage children for life.

Any woman who has had two children born with drugs in their systems or one child born HIV positive should have to appear before a judge. That court could order her to seek medical or drug therapy and counseling. The parent would be informed about birth-control alternatives and, if HIV positive, be given advice about medications such as AZT. If she later became pregnant, she would immediately be compelled to seek further medical aid and counseling. If she refused this counseling and gave birth to a second child with HIV or a third one with drugs in its system, she could be prosecuted and, if found guilty, placed on probation or sent to jail.

Because the children's father frequently walks out, leaving the children and mother more vulnerable, men fathering children born HIV positive or with drugs in their systems should face the same mandatory counseling and probation or jail alternatives as the women.

When I advanced these ideas in the *Times*, the ACLU responded within a week. "We can and should do everything to provide pregnant women with information, prenatal care and therapy for substance abuse or disease. But coercive, punitive policies are . . . counterproductive as a matter of social policy. The 'policing' of pregnancy will only drive troubled pregnant women underground: fearing punishment and the loss of their children, they will avoid seeking the help they need."

The reactions of the ACLU and the judge in Maria's case have much in common. Their responses are propelled by a predetermined philosophy rather than the reality of the situation. Had twelve-year-old Maria come from a middle-class background, I believe the judge would have thrown the book at the thirty-four-year-old Lothario, who would have spent the next several decades as a guest of the Illinois penal system. Or had the defendant been a well-known congressman having sex with a high school junior, the judge might have sent a message to other dirty old men for the benefit of the media and the judge's constitutents. But many judges do not consider twelve-year-old poor kids who have sex with older men victims. These jurists think, that's just how it is with these "people."

The approach I suggested in the HIV/drug case is conservative. Only where a parent refuses counseling can he or she be prosecuted. But the bodily integrity of stupid and abusive parents is so sacred that the ACLU would willingly sacrifice the health, future, and even life of a newborn child—not to mention the exorbitant cost to the taxpayers—on the altar of that philosophy.

I consider myself a liberal. And I'm proud to be a liberal, though I dread the direction in which many so-called liberals have gone. Actually I view the liberal left as reactionary— conservative—because they refuse to question any of their cherished opinions or even consider countervailing evidence.

The sixties were great years to be young, political, and

liberal. Orthodox beliefs unchallenged for decades, even centuries, crumbled before a vigorous and creative onslaught. Liberals were on the cutting edge of this inquiry while conservatives manned the ramparts, protecting the established order. Before long, however, the inquiry became not a means to question beliefs and mores irrelevant to the late twentieth century but an end in itself, a secular religion as ossified and unyielding as the challenged orthodoxy.

The first to feel the wrath of the new self-righteous and infallible liberals were other liberals. To disagree with any aspect of the new liberal liturgy was—is—to be defined as a conservative, fascist, or racist, depending upon the basis of disagreement. Adlai Stevenson, the voice of mid-century American liberalism, would find himself uncomfortable among today's leftists. Accepting the Democratic nomination in 1956, he said, "No man can precisely define liberal without getting into an argument with another liberal. . . . We hold that no doctrine is so sacred that it must reject conflicting evidence. . . . We hold that life is unpredictable, varied and complex, and that those who tell us it is all very simple are lacking either in wisdom or candor. And I hope you will forgive me for reproaching those liberals who regard another's liberalism as genuine only when it coincides with their own opinion on all details of every issue. . . ."

The victim status of the poor, particularly of the black underclass poor, reigns among the most inviolate doctrines in the liberal pantheon. And if someone is a victim, logically someone else has victimized him. That's the rest of us.

By criticizing liberals I do not inferentially suggest that the right holds the answer. If the left is ideologically bankrupt, the right is intellectually dead. If the left too often celebrates the poor as victims, the right as often dismisses them as pariahs. Perhaps the real tragedy of the late twentieth century, probably emanating from the debacle following the Moynihan report, is that left and right ideologues have frozen out the reasonable middle.

Children are best raised by kind and loving parents who are invested in them, or even marginal parents who are more or less invested. For that matter, inadequate parents who occasionally show some semblance of love are better than an underfunded and overextended child welfare system in which a child can be turned to emotional pulp by drifting from foster home to foster home and shelter to shelter. But frequently the choice is not so easy. The child's best interest is the standard in the child welfare arena, but most often we are capable only of avoiding what is in a child's worst interest.

Whether because it is bereft of resources or of hardheaded logic, child welfare has evolved into a brutal system for the object of its ultimate concern, the child. Smart lawyers argue for what a brainwashed and abused seven-year-old child says he wants, though it really reflects what the abuser, the parent, is pushing on the child. Well-intentioned social workers keep kids in shelters or rotating among foster homes in order to prevent the child from being "inappropriately" racially placed. The whole system glorifies, even deifies as victims of poverty those misunderstood "mothers and fathers" who abuse their children. The children, it follows, are victims of a cruel society that victimizes the parents. Child welfare agencies cry out for ever-increasing resources, which means more caseworkers because too many workers in bloated state bureaucracies have burned out but can't be fired because of government unions made greedy and tough by politicians afraid to take them on and enamored of the union's generous political contributions. And the kids sink into oblivion— though of course everyone in the system justifies every act as done in the children's best interest.

Our system of substitute care will never be great. Children are better served when raised by marginal or, at times, even inadequate parents. Now, with the system bursting at its seams, there is more reason than ever to try to keep children in a family atmosphere where possible. But we go much further. We force children to stay with people whose only connection to parenthood is a roll in the hay nine months before the child is born. The time to preserve a family is not when a mother is already thirty years old with five children by different fathers, an eighth-grade education, and no father around to help her or the children.

We must recognize the misery that underclass children endure and the danger they pose for the rest of us in the coming decades. This cancer can only be rooted out by reforming welfare so as to discourage dependency, though there will always be some who will need assistance. We sin today because we have created a fourth-world culture in the midst of the greatest riches the world has ever known, which has unintentionally enslaved many in a culture of dependency, drug abuse, joblessness, and ignorance.

We have the wealth in material resources and brainpower to reverse this problem, if only gradually. But the right lacks commitment and the left reasonableness. The vast center knows something must be done but remains immobilized between the political extremes.

Meanwhile the grandsons of the young black men I prosecuted in 1965 are being sent to prison by the sons and daughters of people I worked with in those years. Many of these felons have graduate-school potential with a ninth-grade reality. They will get out of prison and maybe go back in and lead broken lives, and their sisters have had babies and dropped out of school, and these babies in a few years will have babies and go to jail, and . . .

Index

Index

Index

A NOTE ON THE AUTHOR

Patrick T. Murphy is the Public Guardian of Cook County, Illinois, a position in which he represents abused and neglected children and the elderly disabled. Born in Chicago, he studied at Loyola University in the city and was graduated from the Northwestern University School of Law. Mr. Murphy has been an assistant state's attorney for Cook County, a Peace Corps volunteer, a lawyer with the Legal Assistance Foundation of Chicago, and a lawyer in private practice. His many honors include the Juvenile Justice Award of the American Bar Association and the Criminal Justice Award of the governor of Illinois. He has written a great many articles on juvenile justice and child welfare, and is the author of *Our Kindly Parent the State.* He is married with two sons and lives in Riverside, Illinois.